MCWP 2-2

MAGTF Intelligence Collection

U.S. Marine Corps

PCN 143 000148 00

To Our Readers

Changes: Readers of this publication are encouraged to submit suggestions and changes that will improve it. Recommendations may be sent directly to Commanding General, Marine Corps Combat Development Command, Doctrine Division (C 42), 3300 Russell Road, Suite 318A, Quantico, VA 22134-5021 or by fax to 703-784-2917 (DSN 278-2917) or by E-mail to **nancy.morgan@usmc.mil**. Recommendations should include the following information:

- Location of change
    Publication number and title
    Current page number
    Paragraph number (if applicable)
    Line number
    Figure or table number (if applicable)
- Nature of change
    Add, delete
    Proposed new text, preferably double-spaced and typewritten
- Justification and/or source of change

Additional copies: A printed copy of this publication may be obtained from Marine Corps Logistics Base, Albany, GA 31704-5001, by following the instructions in MCBul 5600, *Marine Corps Doctrinal Publications Status*. An electronic copy may be obtained from the Doctrine Division, MCCDC, world wide web home page which is found at the following universal reference locator: **https://www.doctrine.usmc.mil**.

**Unless otherwise stated, whenever the masculine gender is used, both
men and women are included.**

DEPARTMENT OF THE NAVY
Headquarters United States Marine Corps
Washington, DC 20380-1775

30 July 2004

FOREWORD

Marine Corps Warfighting Publication (MCWP) 2-2, *MAGTF Intelligence Collection*, builds on the doctrinal foundation established by Marine Corps Doctrinal Publication (MCDP) 2, *Intelligence,* and Marine Corps Warfighting Publication (MCWP) 2-1, *Intelligence Operations,* detailing specific doctrine and tactics, techniques, and procedures (TTP) to conduct intelligence collection to support the Marine air-ground task force (MAGTF).

MCWP 2-2 is primarily for intelligence personnel who plan and execute intelligence collection activities. Personnel who support intelligence collection activities or use their results may also find this publication useful.

Reviewed and approved this date.

BY DIRECTION OF THE COMMANDANT OF THE MARINE CORPS

EDWARD HANLON, JR.
Lieutenant General, U.S. Marine Corps
Deputy Commandant for Combat Development
Marine Corps Combat Development Command

Publication Control Number: 143 000148 00

TABLE OF CONTENTS

Page

Chapter 1 Fundamentals

Chapter 2 Collection Requirements Management

Chapter 3 Intelligence Collection Operations Management

Chapter 4 Planning and Execution

Appendices

Figures

CHAPTER 1
FUNDAMENTALS

Intelligence collection is the acquisition of information and the provision of this information to processing elements (Joint Publication [JP] 1-02, *Department of Defense Dictionary of Military and Associated Terms*). In Marine Corps usage, collection is the gathering of intelligence data and information to satisfy the identified requirements (MCRP 5-12C, *Marine Corps Supplement to the Department of Defense Dictionary of Military and Associated Terms*). Successful MAGTF intelligence collection seeks to help reduce uncertainty regarding the enemy, weather, terrain, and operational environment. MAGTF intelligence collection activities form detailed intelligence collection requirements (ICRs), task organic collection assets, and request external collection resources to satisfy the warfighting commander's priority intelligence requirements (PIRs) and other intelligence requirements (IRs).

Intelligence Staff (G-2/S-2) Responsibilities

The intelligence staff (G-2/S-2) has responsibility for intelligence and intelligence operations. The commander relies on the intelligence officer to provide information on weather, terrain, and enemy capabilities, status, and intentions. Through the intelligence annex and supporting appendices, the G-2/S-2 does the following:

- Validates and plans information requirements.
- Coordinates intelligence priorities.
- Integrates collection, production, and dissemination activities.
- Allocates resources.
- Assigns specific intelligence and reconnaissance missions to subordinate elements.
- Supervises the overall intelligence, counterintelligence (CI), and reconnaissance efforts.

See also MCWP 3-40.1, *Marine Air-Ground Task Force Command and Control*, and MCWP 2-1, *Intelligence Operations.*

Specific G-2/S-2 Responsibilities

- Develops and answers outstanding intelligence-related PIRs.
- Prioritizes PIRs and IRs by planning, directing, integrating, and supervising organic multidiscipline MAGTF and supporting intelligence operations.
- Prepares appropriate intelligence, CI, and reconnaissance plans and orders:
  - Reviews and coordinates the all-source intelligence, CI, and reconnaissance plans of joint task forces (JTFs), theaters, and other organizations.
  - Submits and coordinates all-source collection, production, and dissemination requirements beyond the capability of the MAGTF through higher headquarters for JTF, theater or national intelligence support.
- Ensures intelligence information is rapidly processed, analyzed, and incorporated where appropriate in all-source intelligence products, and rapidly disseminates to all MAGTF and external units requiring these.
- Evaluates JTF, theater, and national all-source intelligence support and adjusts stated IRs.
- Identifies deficiencies in intelligence, CI, and reconnaissance personnel and equipment resources.
- Incorporates exercise intelligence in training exercises to improve individual, collective, and unit readiness.
- Facilitates understanding and use of intelligence in support of the planning and execution of operations.

Special Staff Officers under Staff Cognizance of the G-2 Officer

G-2 Operations Officer

The G-2 operations officer has primary responsibility for intelligence support to current and future operations. Specific responsibilities include the following:

- Coordinates and provides intelligence support to the commander, the G-3 operations section, and the rest of the commander's battle staff.
- Serves as the G-2 representative to the MAGTF command element (CE) crisis action team.
- Coordinates, provides, and supervises intelligence support to the MAGTF CE, combat operations center, future operations center, and force fires.
- Plans, directs, and supervises the red cell.
- Provides recommendations on PIR and IR validation, prioritization, and tasking to the G-2 and the intelligence support coordinator (ISC).
- Coordinates and supervises the transition of intelligence planning and operations from G-2 plans to G-2 future operations, and from G-2 future operations to G-2 current operations to effectively support operations.
- Plans, directs, and supervises MAGTF liaison teams to external commands; e.g., the JTF and joint functional components headquarters and intelligence organizations.
- Coordinates with the ISC and MAGTF major subordinate commands' (MSCs') G-2 operations officers for unity of effort of MAGTF intelligence operations.
- Provides intelligence input and other support to MAGTF warning and fragmentary orders (FRAGOs) and to operations-related reporting; e.g., periodic situation reports.
- Coordinates intelligence training for the MAGTF G-2 section and provides G-2 over-sight for and integration of the entire MAGTF intelligence training program.
- Performs other intelligence support and tasks as directed by the G-2.

G-2 Plans Officer

The G-2 plans officer has primary responsibility for intelligence support to the future plans cell. Specific responsibilities include the following:

- Plans the MAGTF concept of intelligence operations for approval by the G-2 and subsequent implementation by the integrated staff cell based on the mission, threat, commander's intent, guidance, and concept of operations.
- Leads, coordinates, and provides intelligence support to G-5 future plans section.
- Plans and coordinates intelligence support requirements for and the deployment of intelligence elements and resources into the area of operations (AO).
- Provides recommendations on PIR and IR validation, prioritization, and taskings to the G-2 and the ISC.
- With the ISC, coordinates G-2 development of Annex B (Intelligence) and Annex M (Geospatial Information and Services) to the operation plan/operation order (OPLAN/OPORD).
- Keeps the G-2 section, other CE staff sections, intelligence liaison personnel, augmentees, and others apprised of MAGTF intelligence planning actions and requirements.
- Identifies requirements and provides recommendations to the G-2 operations officer for MAGTF intelligence liaison teams to external commands; e.g., the JTF or other components' headquarters and intelligence agencies.
- Coordinates and develops policies for intelligence, CI, and reconnaissance operations.
- Plans, directs, and supervises the G-2's imagery and mapping, CI/human intelligence (HUMINT), signals intelligence (SIGINT), and weather sections.

• Performs other intelligence support and tasks as directed by the G-2.

Intelligence Battalion Commander/ISC

The intelligence battalion commander plans, directs, collects, processes, produces, and disseminates intelligence, and provides CI support to the Marine expeditionary force (MEF), MEF MSCs, subordinate MAGTFs, and other commands as directed.

In garrison, the principal task of the intelligence battalion commander is to organize, train, and equip detachments that support MAGTFs or other designated commands to execute integrated collection, intelligence analysis, production, and dissemination of intelligence products.

During operations, the intelligence battalion commander is dual-hatted as the ISC, serving under the direct staff cognizance of the G-2. The S-3 section and the operations center element of the G-2 form the core of the ISC support effort, with planning, direction, and command and control (C2) conducted within the intelligence operation center's (IOC's) support cell. As the ISC, the commander is responsible to the G-2 for the overall planning and execution of all-source intelligence operations. Specific ISC responsibilities during actual operations include the following:

• Implements the concept of intelligence operations developed by the G-2 plans officer and approved by the G-2.
• Establishes and supervises operation of the MAGTF IOC, which includes the support cell, the surveillance and reconnaissance cell (SARC), and the production and analysis (P&A) cell. Generally, the IOC will be collocated with the MAGTF CE's main command post.
• Develops, consolidates, validates, and prioritizes recommended PIRs and IRs to support MAGTF planning and operations. The ISC is tasked to perform PIR and IR validation and prioritization only during actual operations when the IOC is activated. During routine

peacetime operations, PIR and IR validation and prioritization tasks are the responsibility of the G-2 operations officer.

• Plans, develops, integrates, and coordinates intelligence collection, production, and dissemination plans. This includes the effective organic and external integration and employment and staff cognizance of SIGINT; CI; HUMINT; geographic intelligence; imagery intelligence (IMINT); ground remote sensors; ground reconnaissance; and tactical air reconnaissance intelligence collections, production, and dissemination operations.
• Develops (with the G-2 plans officer and G-2 operations officer) and completes Annex B (Intelligence) and Annex M (Geospatial Information and Services) to the OPLAN/OPORD.
• Plans, develops, integrates, and coordinates intelligence and CI support to the commander's estimate; situation development; indications and warning; force protection; targeting; and combat assessment.
• Manages and fuses the threat (or red) common operational picture/common tactical picture (COP/CTP) inputs from subordinate units and external commands and intelligence agencies into the COP/CTP.
• Provides intelligence support to the MAGTF G-2 section and the MSCs.
• Prepares the intelligence and CI estimates to support G-2 plans.
• Plans, develops, and coordinates intelligence communications and information systems (CIS) architecture, including its integration with and support of IMINT and other intelligence and reconnaissance requirements.
• Coordinates and integrates all-source intelligence operations with other Service components; the JTF joint intelligence support element; the theater joint intelligence center or joint analysis center; and national intelligence agencies and operations to include all aspects of intelligence reachback support.
• Assists with the evaluation and improvement of all-source intelligence, CI, and reconnaissance operations.

- Provides other intelligence support and tasks as directed by the G-2.

Collection Management/Dissemination Officer

The collection management/dissemination officer (CM/DO) is sourced from the intelligence battalion's S-3 section and is a key subordinate to the intelligence battalion commander/ISC during operations. The CM/DO forms detailed ICRs and intelligence dissemination requirements (IDRs), and tasking and coordinating internal and external operations to satisfy these. The CM/DO receives validated PIRs and IRs and direction from the ISC, and then plans and manages the best methods to employ organic and supporting collection and dissemination resources through the intelligence collection and dissemination plans.

The CM/DO also validates and forwards national and theater intelligence collection requests from the MAGTF and MSCs typically using appropriate intelligence tools and TTP. He also coordinates intelligence CIS requirements and maintains awareness of available CIS connectivity throughout the MAGTF and with key external organizations. During operations, the CM/DO works within the support cell. In coordination with the P&A cell officer in charge (OIC), the SARC OIC, the G-2 operations officer, the intelligence/reconnaissance commanders, and the G-6, the CM/DO is responsible to the ISC for the following tasks:

- Determines and coordinates the collection effort of PIRs/IRs that may be collected via intelligence, CI, and reconnaissance resources.
- Determines PIRs/IRs and prepares requests for intelligence (RFIs) that are beyond organic capabilities; prepares submissions to higher headquarters and external agencies for support.
- Recommends dissemination priorities, develops intelligence reporting criteria, and advises on and selects dissemination means.
- Uses the Collection Management Board (if established) to develops and coordinates all-source intelligence collection plans, and coordinates and integrates these with MAGTF, other components, JTF, theater, and national intelligence production operations.
- Develops and coordinates all-source intelligence dissemination plans and supporting architectures for voice and data networked communications; coordinates and integrates these with MAGTF, other components, JTF, theater, and national intelligence CIS and dissemination operations.
- Monitors the flow of intelligence throughout the MAGTF; ensures that it is delivered to intended recipients in a timely fashion and satisfactorily meets their needs.
- Evaluates the effectiveness of MAGTF and supporting intelligence collection and dissemination operations.

SARC OIC

The SARC OIC is also an immediate subordinate of the ISC and is responsible for supervising the execution of the integrated organic, attached, and direct support (DS) intelligence collection and reconnaissance operations. The SARC OIC is responsible to the ISC for the following:

- Coordinates, monitors, and maintains the status of all ongoing intelligence, CI, and reconnaissance collection operations. This includes the following:
  - Missions, tasked ICRs, and reporting criteria for all collection missions.
  - Locations and times for all pertinent fire support control measures.
  - Primary and alternate CIS plans for routine and time-sensitive requirements (for collectors and between the collectors or the SARC and key MAGTF CE and MSC C2 nodes) to support ongoing C2 of collection operations and dissemination of acquired data and intelligence to those needing it by the most expeditious means.
- Conducts detailed intelligence collection planning and coordination with the MSCs and intelligence, CI, and reconnaissance organizations'

planners, with emphasis on ensuring understanding of the collection plan and specified intelligence reporting criteria.

- Ensures other MAGTF C2 nodes; e.g., the current operations center or force fires, are apprised of ongoing intelligence, CI, and reconnaissance operations.

- Receives routine and time-sensitive intelligence reports from deployed collection elements; cross-cueing among intelligence collectors, as appropriate; and the rapid dissemination of intelligence reports to MAGTF C2 nodes and others in accordance with IRs, intelligence reporting criteria and dissemination plans, and the current tactical situation.

P&A Cell OIC

The P&A cell OIC's primary responsibility is to manage and supervise the MAGTF's all-source intelligence processing and production efforts. Key responsibilities include the following:

- Plans, directs, and manages operations of the all-source fusion platoon to include the fusion, order of battle, intelligence preparation of the battlespace (IPB), and target intelligence/battle damage assessment (BDA) teams; the topographic platoon; the IMINT platoon; DS teams; and other P&A elements as directed.

- Coordinates and integrates P&A cell operations, estimates, and products with the G-2 section's G-2 operations branch and its red cell operations and estimates.

- Maintains all-source automated intelligence databases, files, workbooks, country studies, and other intelligence studies.

- Plans and maintains imagery, mapping, and topographic resources and other intelligence references.

- Administers, integrates, operates, and maintains intelligence processing and production systems and unclassified general service (message) and sensitive compartmented information systems; e.g., the intelligence analysis system or the image product library.

- Analyzes and fuses intelligence and other information into tailored all-source intelligence products to satisfy all supported commanders' stated or anticipated PIRs and IRs.

- Develops and maintains current and future intelligence situational, threat, and environmental assessments and target intelligence based on all-source analysis, interpretation, and integration.

- Manages and fuses the threat (or red) COP/CTP inputs from subordinate units and external commands and intelligence agencies into the COP/CTP.

For additional information on staff and unit intelligence responsibilities, see MCWP 3-40.1 and MCWP 2-1.

MEF MSC and Unit Responsibilities

Intelligence collection responsibilities also extend to MEF MSCs and units. Key tasks of the MEF MSC intelligence officers include the following:

- Consolidates, validates, and prioritizes MSC IRs and collection needs.

- Submits consolidated requests for external intelligence support.

- Coordinates intelligence activities within their unit.

The unit intelligence officer is generally responsible for the following tasks:

- Coordinates with unit production personnel to verify that the needed information or intelligence is not already available.

- Identifies requirements beyond the unit's capability to satisfy. The unit intelligence section identifies requirements it cannot satisfy internally and forwards these up the chain of command for satisfaction. Detailed justification and the latest time intelligence is of value (LTIOV) should be included so that ICRs can successfully compete with other ICRs for priority collection support.

- Develops unit intelligence collection plans, which must be thoroughly coordinated and integrated with the unit's intelligence production and dissemination plans. Ensures the intelligence plan is responsive to operational needs by analyzing incoming information, determining its value and relevance, and refining future collection needs.
- Integrates collection operations with unit maneuver, fires, communications, and logistics operations. To be effective, collection operations must be coordinated with other operations of the command.
- Plans and supervises operations of organic collection assets and coordinating internal support; e.g., communications, logistics, and security.

MAGTF Intelligence and Reconnaissance Collection Assets

Intelligence data and information are collected by a wide range of MAGTF intelligence and reconnaissance assets. These assets include, but may not be limited to, the following:

- Marine tactical electronic warfare (EW) squadron (VMAQ).
- Radio battalion.
- CI/HUMINT company.
- Ground sensor platoon (GSP).
- Force reconnaissance company.
- Light armored reconnaissance battalion.
- Unmanned aerial vehicle (UAV) squadron.
- Ground combat element reconnaissance battalion/company/platoon.

- Joint surveillance target attack radar system (JSTARS) common ground station.
- F/A-18D reconnaissance capable with advanced tactical airborne reconnaissance system (ATARS).

For additional information on unit capabilities, see the following MCWPs:

- 2-14, *Counterintelligence* (CI/HUMINT).
- 2-15.1, *Remote Sensor Operations* (GSP).
- 2-15.2, *Signals Intelligence* (radio battalion).
- 2-15.4, *Imagery Intelligence* (JSTARS).
- 3-26, *Air Reconnaissance* (F/A-18D ATARS).
- 3-40.5, *Electronic Warfare* (VMAQ and radio battalion).
- 3-42.1, *Unmanned Aerial Vehicle Operations* (UAV).

Intelligence Collection within the Marine Corps Intelligence Cycle

The process used to develop intelligence is called the intelligence cycle. See figure 1-1. The Marine Corps intelligence cycle consists of six sequential yet interdependent steps: planning and direction; collection; processing and exploitation; production; dissemination; and utilization. Collection is the second step, yet collection management is a continuing process and occurs concurrently throughout the cycle. Intelligence collection is a process that helps identify and validate IRs, prioritize them, determine effective means for acquiring information to help satisfy them, and develop, execute, and supervise intelligence and reconnaissance operations.

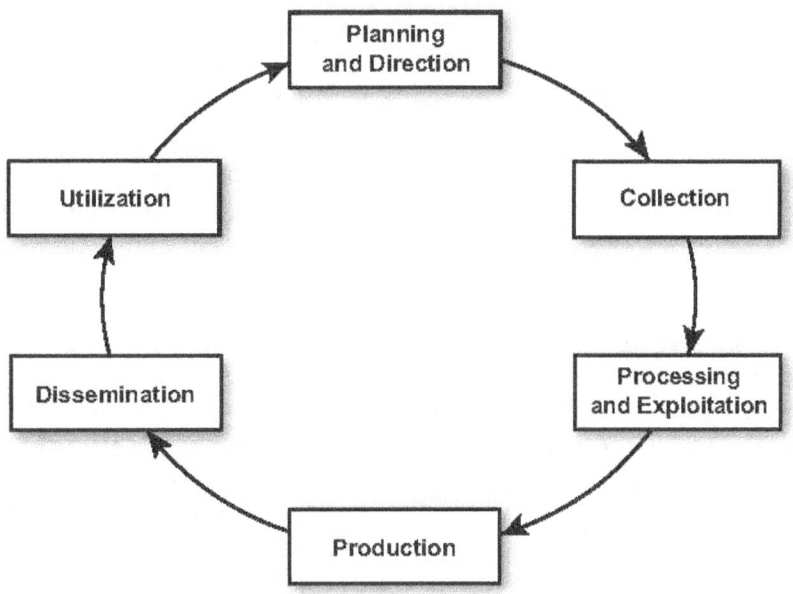

Figure 1-1. The Marine Corps Intelligence Cycle.

Collection Principles

Collection managers may use the following general principles when planning and executing intelligence collection activities. See also JP 2-01, *Joint Intelligence Support to Military Operations*.

Early Involvement

A collection manager must get involved with IRs identification and management early in planning. This ensures thorough consideration and increased flexibility in choosing intelligence collection assets and resources, enhancing the quality and timeliness of collected information.

Prioritization

Prioritization assigns a distinct ranking to each collection requirement. Prioritization must be based on the commander's guidance and the current situation to ensure that assets/resources are directed against the most critical requirements.

Multidiscipline Approach

Collection managers must avoid overreliance on a single collection system or intelligence discipline. Each intelligence collection asset/resource has unique strengths and weaknesses. However, each asset's limitations can be mitigated through the capabilities of other resources. Overreliance on a single asset may result in mission failure if that asset becomes unavailable or the adversary can ascertain its employment pattern and implement countermeasures. A fully integrated collection plan uses collection resources in a complementary manner, adding depth to collection activities.

Task Organic Assets First

Use of organic collection assets allows a timely and tailored response to collection requirements and lessens the burden on collection resources controlled by other units, agencies, and organizations. However, if the requirement cannot be satisfied with organic assets, the collection manager should not hesitate to request external collection support. The collection manager should have an integrated collection plan, including national, theater, and organic collection assets, to ensure ICRs are collected in a timely, accurate manner.

Collection Management Process

Collection management is, in intelligence usage, the process of converting intelligence requirements into collection requirements, establishing priorities, tasking or coordinating with appropriate collection sources or agencies, monitoring results and retasking, as required (JP 1-02). Its purpose is to effectively collect all required intelligence while ensuring the best use of limited and valuable collection assets.

There are two distinct phases of collection management: *collection requirements management (CRM)*, defining what information collections disciplines must collect; and *collection operations management (COM)*, specifying how the collection disciplines will collect. CRM focuses on the IR, is all-source oriented, and generally interacts with intelligence production elements. COM focuses on selecting the specific intelligence disciplines and specific assets to be used to collect information that satisfies IRs. COM establishes a collection strategy and determines how to collect against requirements.

In the MAGTF, CRM and COM are planned, directed, and coordinated by the MAGTF G-2/S-2. However, each MAGTF element has an intelligence staff officer and performs collection management functions. Each unit interacts with levels above and below, and among units, organizations, and agencies on the same level. The further up the chain, the broader the perspective and scope of responsibility and the more organic collection assets and access to collection resources; the lower down the chain, the more specific the function and narrow the scope of collection activities.

CHAPTER 2
COLLECTION REQUIREMENTS MANAGEMENT

Properly articulated, mission-oriented requirements focus the intelligence effort and provide the foundation for successful MAGTF intelligence collection operations.

CRM is the authoritative development and control of collection, processing, exploitation, and/or reporting requirements that normally result in either direct tasking of assets over which the collection manager has authority, or the generation of tasking requests to collection management authorities at a higher, lower, or lateral echelon to accomplish the collection mission (JP 1-02).

CRM focuses on the requirements of the commander, planner or supported units, is oriented at providing all-source intelligence, and generally interacts with intelligence production elements.

CRM organizes, prioritizes, validates, and manages the ICRs that the collection effort must fulfill. CRM is designed to ensure the high priority ICRs get the attention they deserve and determine what specific collection operations and characteristics must be planned and executed to answer these. CRM begins with initial efforts to determine and answer the commander's PIRs established during the planning and direction phase of the intelligence cycle. The compilation of ICRs is the basis for the collection plan. CRM works in cooperation with COM. During CRM a plan is developed to satisfy the requirements, which then transitions to COM for execution. During execution, CRM continues by checking with those supported to determine whether collection operations are actually satisfying their IRs. The CRM process is used to derive, organize, state, and manage IRs.

Requirements Analysis Criteria

IRs are developed as the commanders and staffs work through the Marine Corps Planning Process. Even in the early stages of mission analysis, the collection manager has compiled a number of questions submitted by the staffs and subordinate commanders. In his initial attempts to organize the collection effort, the collection manager analyzes all ICRs he has received. The collection manager helps identify ICRs that can be answered by currently available intelligence and those that will be incorporated in the collection plan. Criteria used to determine the questions that will be converted into collection tasks will be situation-dependent.

Pertinence

Pertinence demands that only ICRs that are relevant to current operations or operations being planned should be planned and executed. Often a proactive commander or staff may submit an ICR in support of an anticipated but not actually assigned follow-on mission or other nonmission-essential task. The collection manager ensures that only relevant ICRs are acted on.

Feasibility

Feasibility demands that only those ICRs that actually can be collected on should be planned and executed. This refers to MAGTF or supporting assets/resources' ability to perform the collection mission, and also to the existence of collectible or "observable" data that the collector will be able to observe, update, and report.

Completeness

Completeness demands that a proposed ICR is complete; i.e., does it ask only one question? The IR should focus on a specific fact, activity or event. The collection manager should identify those questions that are incomplete and coordinate with the originating commander or staff section for refinement. Collection managers must make all efforts to assist commanders and staffs in drafting questions and refining them if returned.

Validation

Validation checks if the proposed ICR has already been answered and/or if it duplicates existing IRs and ICRs. Questions that pass this criterion are said to be "validated." For those not passing this test, collection personnel will initiate coordination with the production element.

Priority

Priority demands that difficult decisions be made regarding the relative importance of some IRs and PIRs compared to others. PIRs must be rank-ordered by the commander in terms of their relative importance to his decisionmaking. There are no "ties" in PIR priorities. If everything is top priority, then effectively nothing is a priority. All IRs that are not designated PIRs but pass all other criteria likewise must be prioritized. The collection manager must prioritize these also, rank-ordering requirements against each other. The collection manager should do the following:

- Always reprioritize dynamically. The collection manager must have a system in place that allows easy reprioritization based on the commander's guidance and tactical needs.
- Keep the commander informed. It is important that the commander knows when a PIR from a subordinate commander will receive lower priority.
- Be prepared to justify priorities. The collection manager must be prepared to explain what factors influenced the prioritization decisions.

Commanders and intelligence officers on other staffs should understand the rationale for the prioritization.

- Continuously communicate current priorities and justifications. Using a database or spreadsheet, subordinate units should be able to monitor the status of their requirements and assess priorities and planned operations. The MAGTF CE should publish and disseminate an updated list as part of an intelligence summary or other periodic product in message format to help lower-echelon commanders and units maintain awareness of higher headquarters' plans and operations. This will also provide an opportunity to adjust for changes in critical situations.

Intelligence Requirements

Intelligence gaps or information needs are formally labeled intelligence requirements. An intelligence requirement is any subject, general or specific, upon which there is a need for the collection of information, or the production of intelligence (JP 1-02). In Marine Corps usage, questions about the enemy and the environment, the answers to which a commander requires to make sound decisions (MCRP 5-12C). IRs drive the collections process and the overall intelligence cycle. IRs are initially developed during the planning process. These are the relevant IRs, related to the enemy, threat or battlespace environment, that commanders deem essential for the successful accomplishment of the mission. IRs are categorized as PIRs and IRs.

PIRs are those intelligence requirements for which a commander has an anticipated and stated priority in the task of planning and decisionmaking (JP 1-02). In Marine Corps usage, an intelligence requirement associated with a decision that will critically affect the overall success of the command's mission (MCRP 5-12C). PIRs are prioritized among themselves and may change in priority over the course of an evolution. Only the commander designates PIRs.

Generally, the difference between a PIR and an IR is that a commander must have the answer to the PIR to make a decision. At any one time there are not many PIRs in effect.

The lowest priority PIR takes precedence over the highest priority IR. IRs are questions typically generated by the staff but not ones that the commander feels he needs answered before making decisions. While there are ideally a few PIRs, there may be many IRs. Like PIRs, IRs should be prioritized against each other to support effective intelligence planning and operations.

PIRs and IRs have the following characteristics. Each PIR or IR—

- Asks only one question.
- Focuses on specific facts, events or activities concerning the enemy or the battlespace.
- Is tied to mission planning, decisionmaking, and execution.
- Provides a clear, concise statement of what intelligence is required.
- Contains geographic and time elements to limit the scope of the requirement.

See also MCWP 2-1.

Requirements Management

Management of IRs is a dynamic process that encompasses the continuous evaluation of the following:

- The importance of each requirement to mission success.
- Continued relevance based upon the current situation and plans.
- Information and assets needed to satisfy each requirement.
- Resources that are presently committed toward fulfilling that requirement.
- The degree to which the requirement has been satisfied by intelligence activities.

Processing IRs

Development of IRs and designation of PIRs is continuous. There is a dynamic flow of new IRs—existing requirements are satisfied or are no longer relevant—and the relative importance of each requirement changes as planning, decisionmaking, execution, and assessment progress. As IRs are developed, the collection manager validates, refines, and enters them into the collection management system.

Validating IRs

Validation ensures that the IR is relevant to the mission, has not already been satisfied, and does not duplicate any other requirements.

Refining IRs

Refining the IR entails placing it in the proper format, identifying all related information components, and adding appropriate qualifiers such as geographic limitations or time constraints. During refinement, similar or related IRs may be combined into a single, comprehensive IR.

Managing IRs System

A requirements management system is an essential tool that provides a means to monitor the effort to satisfy each IR. Each intelligence section must develop a system appropriate to its mission and echelon. Minimal components of any IR management system follow:

- A numbering system.
- Identifying who submitted the requirement.
- Designating collection and production assets committed to satisfying the IR or noting when the IR was submitted to higher headquarters or supporting agencies, if organic assets are not available.
- Timeliness requirements.
- Dissemination instructions and information.
- A mechanism to track user satisfaction.

Reviewing Priorities

The collection manager must continually reassess the emphasis given to each IR and realign the priorities according to the commander's intent, current situation, and the planning cycle phase. The intelligence officer must also periodically confirm the assignment of priorities with the commander to ensure that the intelligence effort is focused in accordance with the commander's desires. In addition to IRs of his own command, the collection manager usually receives requests for information from outside agencies (subordinate, adjacent, and senior). Given that MAGTF intelligence operations are centrally managed by the MAGTF CE, the collection manager must continually solicit, assess, and integrate the IR needs of subordinate commanders.

Satisfying IRs

Once an IR has been identified, validated, refined, and prioritized, the collection manager must determine how to satisfy it and allocate the appropriate intelligence and reconnaissance assets to obtain the desired information and intelligence. If the IR cannot be satisfied by organic assets, it must be submitted to higher headquarters or supporting forces/agencies for satisfaction. In determining how to satisfy an IR, the collection manager must consider each step in the intelligence cycle to ensure that the plan encompasses the entire process from collection through utilization. In conjunction with the P&A cell OIC and the CM/DO, the collection team must identify the information needed, where and how to get it, how to package the intelligence into an appropriate product, and how to deliver that product.

Normally, an IR will generate tasks to collect data or information; process/produce tactical intelligence to answer the question; and disseminate the intelligence to all users needing it by a specific time.

Organizing the Collection Effort Around Requirements

Each IR will generally have an associated ICR, intelligence production requirement (IPR), and IDR. See figure 2-1. However, in practice, an intelligence development effort is rarely concentrated on a single IR. Normally, related IRs are grouped together and synchronized to ensure that intelligence operations are focused on the PIRs and satisfy as many IRs as possible. This grouping also helps with the need to employ intelligence resources in the most effective and efficient manner.

Assets/resources to requirements must be matched. Once the ICRs, IPRs, and IDRs have been identified, the intelligence officer allocates the necessary collection, processing and exploitation, production, and dissemination assets to carry out the task.

Collection agencies and production requirements must be assigned. The remainder of the planning and direction effort entails managing the intelligence effort to ensure that intelligence assets stay focused on the PIRs and that the results are being delivered and used to effect tactical decisions. Principles of assigning collection agencies and analytical production to requirements include the following:

- Requirement research: to ensure previously acquired/developed intelligence does not answer current requirements, to include exploiting ongoing/planned collection operations of other friendly forces.

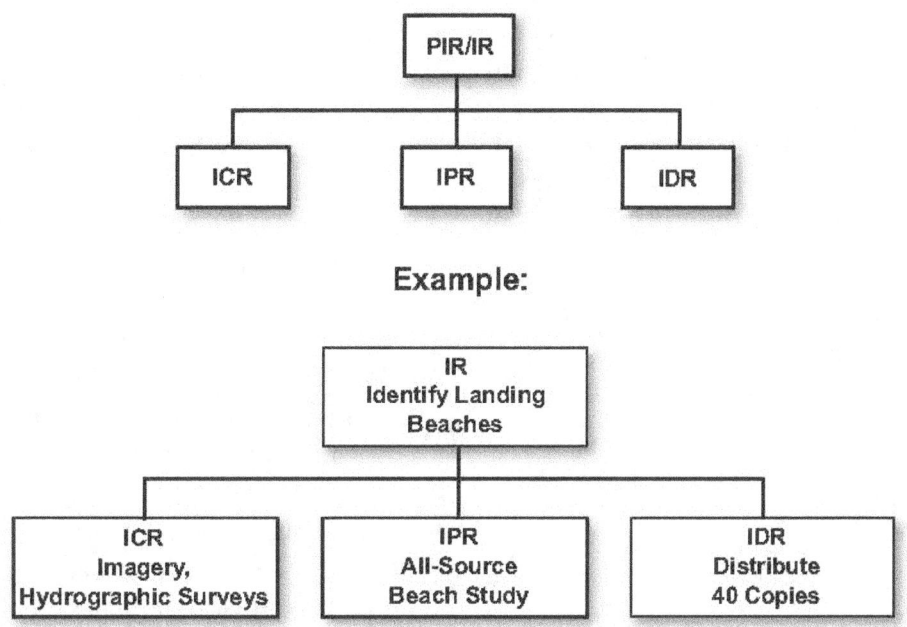

Figure 2-1. Requirements Satisfaction.

- Assessing collectability of the target versus available sensors and other collectors. This identifies the capability of the asset/resource to collect and suitability of the asset/resource to collect. Often what is marginally capable is not necessarily the most suitable to collect, but might be tasked if necessary.

- Conceptualizing multiplicity of collection: to ensure redundancy and as a hedge in case of single asset/resource or single collections discipline failure.

ICR Development Process

The ICR development process uses a building block approach of four steps that translates broad questions into concrete questions, tasks, and orders for collection agencies to perform. See figure 2-2.

Step 1, Identify, Validate, and Prioritize PIRs and IRs

This is the foundation of the ICR development process. It is the basis for collection planning and execution. A common mistake in regard to PIRs

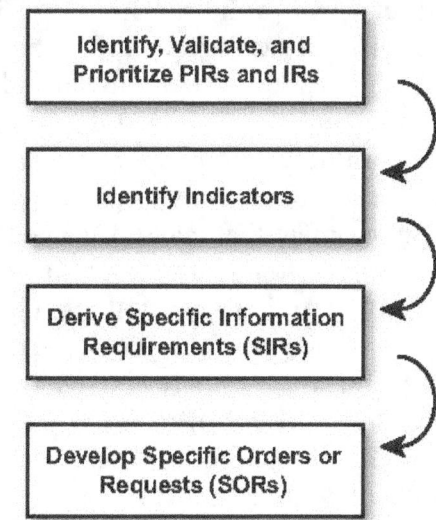

Figure 2-2. ICR Development Process.

and IRs in general is that they lack adequate specificity. Poorly developed PIRs increase the potential of failure regarding timely, pertinent collection, and follow-on intelligence operations. Focused, specific requirements are needed to make informed, effective plans and decisions. Below are examples of common PIRs, with an evaluation of each one's effectiveness.

PIR 1: "Where is the enemy going to attack?" This PIR is too broad, leaving too much open to interpretation in terms of critical considerations, such as specific—

- Threat unit.
- Threat equipment.
- Threat activity.
- Place and time.

PIR 2: "Will the enemy tank division attack our Obj A along Highway 66 prior to D-2?" This PIR provides enough specificity to enable effective collection of the required information and shows how to write a good IR.

Step 2, Identify Indicators

Once the critical IR question has been determined, the next step is to identify the activities that will confirm (or help deny if missing) the event specified in each PIR and IR. These activities, called indicators, are usually stated in general terms, such as "forward deployment of artillery." Indicators provide positive or negative evidence of threat activity or a characteristic of the environment that may influence the commander's selection of a particular course of action (COA). An indicator will often be associated with a named area of interest (NAI), which is a geographical area where activity is expected to occur that will confirm or deny an enemy COA. Guiding principles for indicator development follow:

- Collect on environment conditions or indicators. Developing an indicator related to a characteristic of the environment may be difficult because often there is no activity that describes

a characteristic of the AO. It may be useful to evaluate these kinds of indicators in terms of a condition rather than an activity.

- Indicators must be focused and specific. Good requirements, whether PIRs or IRs, ask only one question, focusing on a specific fact, event or activity. The intelligence analyst uses indicators to correlate particular events or activities that occur—or fail to occur—to determine probable enemy COAs.

- Don't overlook the value of negative results. Negative information can be as important as positive information. Negative or disconfirming evidence can provide the intelligence analyst insight about the enemy's rejection of a COA. Negative information could lead to further investigation of a possible branch COA.

Step 3, Derive Specific Information Requirements

Each PIR/IR generates sets of associated specific information requirements (SIRs). SIRs are the observable or "collectible" bits of information that describe the information required to answer all or part of an ICR. A completed SIR describes the information required, the location where the required information can be collected, and the timeframe when it can be collected.

Drafting SIRs is an analytical, time-consuming process requiring a thorough understanding of the particular PIR or IR.

Marine Corps Intelligence Activity (MCIA) 1540-002-95, *Generic Intelligence Requirements Handbook (GIRH)*, facilitates rapid, time-sensitive, crisis intelligence planning for MAGTFs. The GIRH is a compendium of frequently asked IRs, organized by mission profile, orders of battle, and terrain. The GIRH is used primarily as a checklist to rapidly organize planning and to determine gaps in information. It may be used as a sort of brevity code to efficiently request information. It may also be used as a baseline intelligence support tool for intelligence centers providing operational intelligence to forward deployed forces. The GIRH is not a stand-alone substitute for SIR development. Collection managers should not "cut and paste" lists of requirements from the GIRH into their collection requirements list without going through the IR development criteria.

Having linked IRs to an indicator, that indicator must be broken down into very specific questions. This process consists of identifying the specific sets of information that will provide an answer—partial or complete—to each IR. Steps for developing SIRs include the following:

- Further narrow the focus of each indicator to identify "where to collect" (tying it to a specific point on the battlefield). We may use a specific NAI to replace the general idea of "forward" in the indicator, "forward deployment of artillery" and rewrite it as "artillery deployed in NAI 12."

- Refine the time to be observed. Starting from the LTIOV, collections personnel plan backward to determine collection times, taking into account time requirements to sort through collected data, report it, process it, analyze it, and further disseminate it to those needing it. If no LTIOV is specified, it must be requested from the originator of the requirement.

- Determine the specific observables. Next consider the "what to collect," building more detail by identifying the specific information that supports the indicator. For example, the specific information that supports the indicator, "artillery deployed in NAI 12," might include the presence of the following:
  - Artillery weapons.
  - Fire direction control equipment or vehicles.
  - Artillery-associated communications equipment.
  - Artillery ammunition carriers.

- Complete the SIR. A complete SIR describes the information required, the location where the required information can be collected, the time when it can be collected, reporting criteria, and principal and secondary recipients. Generally, each IR generates sets of SIRs.

- Refine the SIR. Develop each indicator further by identifying the specific types of equipment or other collectible/observable characteristic associated with each SIR. For example, replace—
  - "Artillery weapons" with specifics such as "120mm mortars" or "107mm multiple rocket launcher battery," if that is what should be present within the NAI and enemy force composition.
  - "Artillery-associated communications" with "the ABC data signal," if that is the type used by the enemy unit in question. This specificity will aid the collection or asset managers to optimize their collection capabilities against the target in question.

These SIRs have been properly developed. The collection manager has taken a focused PIR, matched indicators to it, i.e., activities that will confirm an event specified in the intelligence requirement, and developed SIR sets to support focused collection. A well-developed IR will contain all information needed to develop supporting SIRs. In this case, the IR often states the "where" and "when" to collect; the requirements manager needs only to refine the "what to collect" into specific items of information. A poorly developed SIR often results in requirements that do not contain the information needed to identify "where" and "when" to collect. Further coordination with the requester of information is then needed to obtain the "where and when." The following scenario is an example of identifying the previous steps of developing SIRs.

During wargaming, a regimental commander tells the S-2 "In order to commit our reserve I need to know if that tank regiment will turn east or west at Tonbak." The collection manager refines this into the PIR "Will the 3d Tank Division enter NAI 8 or NAI 9 on the evening of 5 May?" (triggers regimental reserve)

Note how the PIR is tied to a decision. The results of collection, i.e., the friendly responses, are stated as a *decision trigger*. The IR, as received and worded, is a good one for beginning focused requirements development. It already contains a reasonably detailed description of *what* the commander needs to know, *where* to find the intelligence, and *when* the event is expected to occur. However, the CRM needs to supply the COM and collection mission planners with more detail to support their planning and the subsequent development of SORs. Thus, the CRM concentrates on identifying good indicators to confirm or deny the information desired. One indicator is "movement south of the enemy's 3d Tank Division." The collection manager then develops the following sets of SIRs designed to support the *same* PIR:

- "Will more than 220 combat vehicles of the 3d Tank Division pass through NAI 8 or NAI 9 between 051400 and 060400 March?"
- "Will more than 17 reconnaissance vehicles subordinate to the 3d Tank Division or its regiments pass through NAI 8 or NAI 9 between 041800 and 052000 March?"
- "Will more than 38 artillery weapons subordinate to the 3d Tank Division enter NAI 8 or NAI 9 between 015200 and 060200 March?"
- "Are more than 2 R-XYZ radios active in NAI 8 or NAI 9 before 060200 March?"

Step 4, Develop SORs

Each indicator generates a number (sets) of SIRs. Each SIR will, in turn, generate a SOR that can be used to task collection assets or request collection resource support from external assets in the COM process. A well-written SIR is easily translated into an effective SOR by making a directive vice inquisitive statement. In other words, if a SIR is a question, the SOR directs a collection asset or resource to find an answer.

A SOR is the order or request that generates planning and execution of a collection mission or analysis of database information and intelligence. SORs sent to subordinate commands, to include collection assets, are orders. SORs sent to other commands, usually collection resources, are requests. After SORs have been developed, the collection manager is ready to develop the collection plan. The collection plan will reflect the SORs assigned to selected collectors for each IR.

Avoid overly restrictive reporting criteria and guidelines. Allowing collectors appropriate latitude will enable them to provide not only the requested information, but possibly other valuable information not specifically requested. A sample SIR follows.

SIR: "Will more than 17 reconnaissance vehicles subordinate to the 3d Tank Division or its regiments pass through NAI 8 or NAI 9 between 041800 and 052000 May? LTIOV: 052000 May."

SOR 1A: "Report the presence of reconnaissance vehicles in NAI 8 or NAI 9 between 041800 and 052000 May. Specify direction of movement and numbers and types of vehicles. LTIOV: 052000 May."

SOR 1B: "Report the presence of communications nodes associated with reconnaissance elements of the 3d Tank Division or its subordinate regiments in NAI 8 or NAI 9 between 041800 and 52000 May. LTIOV: 052000 May."

Collection Assets/Resource Selection Factors

After defining ICRs and supporting SIRs/SORs, the collection manager must determine the availability and capability of collection assets and resources that may contribute to ICR satisfaction. The collection manager compares the characteristics of the target with the specific aspects of the requirement and the characteristics of available assets or resources to determine the collectors to select. This step involves a cooperative and coordinated effort for both the CRM and COM processes.

The four basic factors that influence selection are capability, suitability (or feasibility), redundancy/multiplicity, and balance. Other factors to consider are target key elements, collection capabilities, correlation, and the environment.

Capability

Is the asset/resource physically and technically capable of collecting the required information on the particular target of interest within the limitations imposed by the requirement? To decide if an asset or resource can collect the data, the collection manager considers a range of operational and technical factors that include key element sets of the target, geography, weather conditions, and threat activity. These factors are then correlated or compared to asset and/or resource availability and capability factors; e.g., platform and sensor range, preparation and system timeliness or characteristics of sensor.

Suitability (or Feasibility)

Is the asset/resource actually suitable to perform the mission, whether alone or in combination with other collectors? The collection manager determines if the different collection/intelligence disciplines have a high confidence level of successfully executing assigned missions given their unique capabilities and limitations. These capabilities and limitations are generally focused on technical or performance characteristics, range, dwell time, and timeliness.

Redundancy/Multiplicity

Should another collector be tasked to collect against the same requirement to provide redundancy or to pose a detection dilemma for the enemy? In some cases a collection asset or resource may not be able to fully satisfy a requirement. To achieve a greater degree of satisfaction, the collection manager employs redundancy of tasking to other collectors. Redundancy employs a collection strategy that involves the use of several same-discipline assets to cover the same target. Redundancy is used on high priority targets when the probability of any one system adequately collecting is low. The collection manager also mixes different sensors in different intelligence disciplines to achieve combined arms effects on an enemy target.

Balance

Are any collection assets/resources overtasked and others underutilized? Proper balance ensures the efficient tasking and employment of all organic and supporting intelligence and reconnaissance assets without overburdening/overcommiting any or underusing others.

Target Key Elements

Key element sets are the parameters of the target's characteristics that can be compared with characteristics of the available collection assets and/or resources to serve as discriminators in discipline or sensor selection. The key elements commonly considered are target characteristics, range to the target, and timeliness.

Target characteristics are the discernible physical, operational, and technical features of a unit, object, event or other intelligence target. These characteristics may be observable and collectible. Observables are the unique descriptive features associated with the visible description (or signature) of the target, whether it is specific units, equipment or facilities. Collectibles are unique descriptive features associated with emanations from the target. Observables are associated with emanations via IMINT, HUMINT, CI and ground/air reconnaissance; collectibles with SIGINT and CI; both associated with measurement and SIGINT.

Range is measured as distance from a predetermined reference point to the target location. The range to the target can be used to quickly eliminate from consideration those standoff sensors that cannot cover the target area and those sensors on penetration platforms that cannot reach the target area.

Timeliness refers to a comparison of the demonstrated system timeliness of a collection asset or system with the time the ICR must be satisfied by the published LTIOV.

Collection Capabilities

The collection manager translates the capabilities and limitations of available collectors into a set of collection capability factors that can be directly compared to the key target element sets. The capabilities and limitations of the various collectors are considered, together with their availability, to determine if they should be tasked. Sensor capability factors are technical or performance characteristics, range, dwell time, and timeliness.

Performance characteristics are concerned with the system's ability to collect the needed information, output quality, and geolocational accuracy. A collector within a particular discipline may or may not be able to collect information on a particular target. The data quality relates to the level of detail derived from the collected information; e.g., different imagery systems provide varying degrees of imagery resolution. The importance of geolocational accuracy depends on the planned use of the information collected; e.g., targeting demands greater locational accuracy than information collected for threat unit identification and order of battle updates.

Range deals with the collector's ability to provide target coverage. For airborne systems, range is determined by considering the actual range capabilities of the aircraft and its collection system to provide detailed information sufficient to satisfy the requirement and any operational or fire support restrictions placed on it. The CRM process assesses combinations of these range factors to determine the collector's potential to meet the tactical ICR.

Dwell time is the length of time a given collector can maintain access to the target, an important consideration during collection monitoring, particularly during high tempo operations.

Timeliness considers the time required to complete each collection event and is calculated or estimated for each available sensor based on the tactical situation. Times vary depending on mission priority assigned, specific system availability, time required to plan the mission, and related information processing and dissemination means. These times are added to find an overall elapsed time, then compared with the latest timeliness information stated by the requirement originator.

Correlation

Correlation is the process that associates and combines independent data on a single subject to improve collection reliability or credibility. Key target element sets are compared with collection capability factors to provide a preliminary list of units and sensors that are technically able to collect the desired data within range to the target and time required.

Environment

After correlation, candidate sensors are compared with environmental factors to support final sensor selection. Environmental factors include collector vulnerability to the threat, weather and light conditions, and terrain that might influence the collector's ability to acquire the necessary information. Depending on the environment, a technically capable sensor may be dropped from consideration.

Sensor vulnerability is the degree to which adversary fires countermeasures (deception, camouflage, and operations security) will affect sensor selection and depends on the vulnerability of the sensor platform. In general, the platforms of penetrating sensors are the most vulnerable, stand-off sensors less so, and satellite sensors the least vulnerable. Threat assessment is an evaluation of risk versus potential intelligence gain.

Weather and light conditions are considerations, particularly with imagery and visual collection sensors. Weather conditions in and around the target area affect the sensor capability to collect and exploit data.

Terrain is also a consideration. It may mask a target, thereby dictating the direction a sensor must point or locate, which will influence ingress/egress route planning for penetration sensors, flight paths, loiter tracks for standoff sensors and/or satellites, SIGINT collection/direction finding site selection or additional radio communications relay needs.

Intelligence Collection Planning

Compilation of ICRs and SIRs is the basis of the collection plan. Collection planning is defined as a continuous process that coordinates and integrates the efforts of all collection assets and resources. The CRM cycle begins with initial efforts to answer the IRs, particularly the commander's PIRs, established during the planning and direction phase of the intelligence cycle. Based on these requirements, intelligence analysts prepare RFIs. In the context of collection management, RFIs are queries to see if the information and intelligence already exists. If not, they form the basis for the ICRs and IPRs. When the RFI manager positively determines that the information is neither available nor extractable from archived information or from other intelligence sources, an intelligence gap is identified. It then becomes the responsibility of the collection manager to obtain the information.

The collection plan includes the supported IRs, SIRs, when the information is needed, reporting criteria, who is to receive the finished intelligence, and how it is to be used. The information collected to satisfy these ICRs will answer the IR or be used in intelligence analysis and production. The collection plan forms the basis for further collection actions. The collection plan is integrated and coordinated, selecting the best collectors to satisfy each requirement. It will be a text, graphic or combined representation of the collection strategy. The collection plan may be a simple hardcopy or automated worksheet used solely by the intelligence section, or a more formal, comprehensive document, depending on the complexity of the requirements to be satisfied. Regardless of whether automated or manual tools are used, the basic content of the collection plan includes the following:

- IRs.
- Indicators.
- SIRs.
- Collection assets and resources to be employed.
- Reporting criteria and instructions.
- Remarks.

IRs Worksheet

The IRs worksheet is a useful tool for tracking the status of IRs. The format is established by unit procedures or may be established within the OPLAN/OPORD. See figure 2-3 on page 2-12 and appendix A for a detailed description.

MEF IR Number	Requester Number	DTG Received	Subject	Action	Status
04-1012	1st Marine Division Number 04-001	090830 Jan	Recon Activity in NAI 32	SOR Numbers 04-1462 (UAV) 04-1463 (GSP) 04-1464 (Force Reconnaissance)	Closed 091630 Jan
04-1014	MEF G-2/P&A Cell	101100 Jan	Imagery of landing beaches	Forwarded to JTF J-2 or national collection	Pending

Figure 2-3. Sample Intelligence Requirements Worksheet.

Intelligence Collection Worksheet

The intelligence collection worksheet is a useful tool for linking IRs to collection assets. The format is established by unit procedures or may be established within the OPLAN/OPORD. See appendix B for a sample intelligence collection worksheet.

Reporting

Specific reporting criteria instructions are included. Normally, the place where information is reported is the unit that submitted the requirement.

Collection and Related Planning Tools

Although the collection management process has been formalized for quite some time, it remains dynamic and continually evolving. Technological advances have increased the timeliness of collections planning, direction, and execution. Many collection planning tools have emerged that provide significant improvements to the process. The most important of these follow:

- Standard collection plan format. The collection plan establishes guidance for intelligence collection activities and tasks collection assets. See appendix C for a sample intelligence collection plan. It contains specific orders for subordinate elements to collect and report information.
- Collection tasking worksheet. This management tool assists the collection manager in identifying a specific collector, system or discipline best suited to collect against a particular information requirement. See figure 2-4.

COLLECTION TASKING WORKSHEET

Organization: Registration:

DTG: Collection Manager:

SIRs:

Time: Target Range:

Characteristics:

Assets/ Resources	Range	Timeliness	Characteristic	Weather	Geography	Threat	Capability	Remarks
HUMINT								
CI								
IMINT								
COMINT								
ELINT								
MASINT								
OSINT								

Assets/Resource Selected:	HUMINT:	COMINT:	MASINT:	CI:
	IMINT:	ELINT:	OSINT:	

Figure 2-4. Intelligence Collection Tasking Worksheet.

- IPB collection techniques. When properly conducted, the results of IPB are an exceptional aid in identifying critical gaps of information and focusing collection requirements. The event template and event matrix together describe the indicators and activity expected to occur in NAIs, targeted areas of interest, and decision points. Using the decision support template and a graphical or written record of COA wargaming, the collection manager can determine where collection is required, what is to be collected, and when the information is required.

- Collection status update paragraph. The use of collection status update paragraphs as part of an intelligence summary is an effective technique to ensure all within the MAGTF are aware of planned collection missions. In it the collection manager provides a summary of the unit's collection priorities and planned operations for a specified period. The collection status paragraph can update a unit's active and cancelled requirements, and is a good way to inform subordinate, adjacent, and higher headquarters units of the a MAGTF's planned collection requirements and operations. Appendix D provides an example of a collection status update paragraph to a MEF intelligence summary. Items that may be included are intelligence collection priorities, cancelled requirements, and planned intelligence collection missions.

Intelligence and Reconnaissance Assets Tasking

The tasking mechanism for MAGTF intelligence and reconnaissance assets is situation-dependent and shaped by a number of variables. The collection manager issues orders to those assets that are in DS or attached to his unit. Certain external collection resources are tasked only through structured and rigorously enforced standards for collection requests; e.g.,

national IMINT and SIGINT systems. The intent of these collections tasking guidelines is to standardize the process to improve the quality and timeliness of collection operations.

Standard Formats for Asset Tasking

Tasking request formats or messages depend on the tactical situation, type of sensor, and type of asset or resource; i.e., organic, supporting, theater, national or multinational. Many specific data elements in these requests and the transmission procedures are classified. In the case of MAGTF organic and DS, requesters follow combatant command instructions provided in the unit standing operating procedures (SOPs), theater procedures, and OPLAN/OPORD intelligence annexes. The Joint Tactical Exploitation of National Systems manual and the 58-series of the Defense Intelligence Agency Manuals (DIAMs) provide guidance for requesting collection support from national resources.

Guidelines for Requesting National/Theater Collection Support

Formats to request national and theater collection are in various DIAMs (58-series), Joint Tactical Exploitation of National Systems manual, and combatant and theater command TTP. Regardless of the formats used or the mechanisms for tasking those national/theater resources, CRM should be guided by the following principles:

- Areas of interest. National systems are best employed against high-priority targets outside the range of organic or theater sensors, beyond standoff collection range, and/or in high areas.
- Exploitation and/or analysis timeliness. Targets must be chosen such that, under applicable timeliness constraints, exploitation reports will reach the commander in time to react or influence decisionmaking.

- Justifications. Request justifications must fully explain the need for information and support the priority assigned by the requester.
- Sensor capabilities. Target descriptions must place minimum restrictions on the employment of collection systems.
- Sensor accessibility. The targets' accessibility must be determined when possible before a collection request is forwarded.
- Exploitation and/or analysis requirements clarity (concise, explicit statements of actual information needed).
- Exploitation and/or analysis requirement purpose (state the purpose of the information desired when it will benefit the interpreter and/or analyst).
- Preplanned collection. Preplanned target sets submitted in advance of an operation can relieve the workload and must be considered where the tactical situation permits.

Production Requests

Once the unit intelligence officer determines that the requirement cannot be met with local resources, the requirement is forwarded up the chain of command for satisfaction. The intelligence officer determines whether to submit the requirement as RFI, ICR, IPR or production request (PR).

Generally, an RFI is submitted if the requirement is a fairly straightforward question. In a noncombatant evacuation operation, an RFI may be, "How many personnel require evacuation?" In this case, no extensive collection or production is required because the intelligence is generally available.

A PR is more appropriate when the IR is complex or substantial; e.g., "What is the capability of country X to defend its coastline against an amphibious assault?" This requirement may result in an IPR for the MEF CE or a PR to the JTF headquarters because the answer will require the collection and analysis of a large amount of

information ranging from hydrographic conditions to available threat weapon systems. Such analysis may be beyond the capabilities of a small unit intelligence section and more appropriately performed at the theater or Service level where access to information and ability to task collection resources are greater.

A PR is also appropriate to satisfy a requirement that may be recurring in nature or in a denied area; e.g., "How many aircraft are maintained on alert status at airfield Y?" If organic assets are not available, the unit intelligence officer will submit a request for theater and national production assets to monitor the airfield to determine the answer. As an RFI travels up the chain of command, it is satisfied (from available information or intelligence or by collecting new data), converted into a PR or forwarded to the next higher level for satisfaction. Each unit in the chain of command validates the PR and satisfies it from within or passes the requirement to the next higher authority for action.

Most IPRs are levied on the intelligence battalion, P&A company's P&A cell, which is the MAGTF's principal deliberate production asset. Based on the commander's guidance and the G-2/S-2's direction, the intelligence battalion commander or ISC does the following:

- Plans, manages, and conducts MAGTF IPR management.
- Exercises staff cognizance over MEF collection and production elements to fulfill PRs.
- Determines PRs that are produced locally and PRs that are forwarded to the appropriate theater, Service or national Department of Defense Intelligence Production Program (DODIPP) production center validation officer (VO).

The VO reviews the PR, determines if to accept and satisfy it, forward to another production center or invalidate the PR. The combatant commander, the joint force commander or the MAGTF commander directs PR and RFI procedures, which vary from theater to theater; e.g., a

MAGTF preparing to deploy submits PRs through the normal Service chain of command to the MCIA VO. However, a MAGTF operationally assigned to a combatant commander submits PRs through the established operational chain of command to the VO supporting that theater. A theater intelligence directorate (J-2) may delegate validation authority to a JTF J-2 during a crisis, providing the JTF J-2 a streamlined path for joint intelligence center production support and priority over other noncrisis production requirements. For most crises and contingencies, annex B to the joint force commander's OPLAN/OPORD specifies policies and procedures for requesting intelligence production support.

Production Request Format

The same basic format is generally used for RFIs and PRs. This facilitates conversion of an RFI into a PR at a later time. A basic level PR must include the following:

- Organizations and specific offices or individuals requesting the product.

- A statement describing the required information and intelligence and sources consulted by the requester and source shortcomings relative to the request.
- LTIOV.
- Product form; e.g., hardcopy text, electronic file on disk, and total quantity of each.
- Requirements prioritization for multiple elements.

The basic format is sufficient at lower tactical levels. At higher levels the format becomes more structured. Defense Intelligence Management Document 0000-151C-95, *Department of Defense Intelligence Production Program (DODIPP): Production Procedures*, stipulates the format for PRs, which ultimately will be forwarded to a DODIPP VO and production center. Each combatant command defines formats and procedures in their applicable intelligence procedure documents. The MEF CE and MSC headquarters SOP define formats for their headquarters and subordinate elements. See also MCWP 2-12, *MAGTF Intelligence Production and Analysis*.

CHAPTER 3
INTELLIGENCE COLLECTION OPERATIONS MANAGEMENT

Collection operations management is the authoritative direction, scheduling, and control of specific collection operations and associated processing, exploitation, and reporting resources. (JP 1-02)

The COM process organizes, directs, and monitors the units, equipment, and personnel that actually collect the data to satisfy the ICRs. Strategies and plans are developed for collection to accomplish the following:

- Estimate how well a collection asset or resource can satisfy requirements.
- Evaluate the performance of collection assets and resources.
- Allocate and task assets or request resources.
- Monitor and report the results and status of collection efforts, organizations, and systems.

Actions taken by units explicitly to satisfy IRs are collection operations. Considerations are similar to any other kind of operation. Intelligence COM is concerned with the mission management (how to employ collection resources) and asset management (execution of collection missions) functions of the collection cycle and includes the following:

- Mission planning and collection plan development.
- Collection asset tasking.
- Exploitation and reporting.
- Supervision of the collection effort.
- Updating the collection plan during execution.

Mission Planning and Collection Plan Development

Mission planning is based on the requirements generated by the CRM process. It plans and executes operations to satisfy those requirements. It supports the entire intelligence cycle, focusing on the processing and exploitation, production, and dissemination steps of the intelligence cycle and the collection process. As an integral step in the CRM/COM process, the collection manager must be informed of the requirement originator's guidance for production and dissemination. Any specific constraints or restraints should be identified during the CRM process and factored into COM mission planning.

COM mission planning is concerned with identifying, scheduling, and controlling collection assets and/or resources. The COM planner reviews the mission requirements for system responsiveness, weather, threat data, and intelligence reporting requirements. These elements are considered with the detailed technical, CIS, administrative, and logistical data of each tasked asset or collection system to determine asset availability and capability. Requirements are then translated into specific mission tasking orders.

CRM and COM processes use similar intelligence collection planning and management tools including the following:

- Intelligence collection worksheet.
- Intelligence collection plan.
- Collection reports.
- Collection status update paragraph.
- Collection emphasis message.

In simple terms, COM allocates and tasks assets and resources and monitors and reports the status of collection operations.

Collection Asset Tasking

Key considerations that affect the planning and scheduling of intelligence collection operations follow:

- Clear communication of mission, intent, concept of operations, and tasks to those units that must execute them.
- Ensuring suitability of intelligence collection resources to accomplish missions and achieve objectives, to include that of the unit and all subordinate and supported commands.
- Ensuring sustainability of intelligence collection operations to support current and anticipated future operations.
- Monitoring progress of intelligence collection operations and adjusting plans to achieve collection objectives.

While much of the responsibility for most of overall planning and direction effort rests with the G-2/S-2's intelligence operations officer, the collection manager must maintain concurrent awareness of these factors and their impact on collection planning and operations.

After a thorough study of availability, capability, and performance history, the collection manager selects the resource most capable to satisfy the requirement. Various approaches to collection exist. They center around three strategies or a combination of them:

- Tasking organic or supporting intelligence and reconnaissance resources.

- Requesting intelligence and reconnaissance collection support from external MAGTF forces.
- Recommending other collection tasking to subordinate elements.

Tasking Organic Collections and Production Assets or Supporting Collection and Production Resources

Although the strategy adopted by the collection manager will always vary based on the mission and the IRs to be satisfied, tasking organic assets should be considered first. The advantage to this is that the collection manager has the most control over these assets and they are generally more responsive. The collection manager usually understands their capabilities, limitations, and performance history well. Generally, reconnaissance assets should not be held in reserve. A possible exception to the policy of employing all reconnaissance assets without a reserve is when the collection manager is aware of a future requirement that will need to be addressed.

Requesting Support from External MAGTF Collection and Production Resources

The IRs generated in the planning cycle often mandate employment of external resources. When selected, requests for support from higher headquarters, e.g., JTF, theater or national assets, should be prepared and submitted up the chain of command. Although external collection resources may be more capable than some organic assets, the collection manager runs the risk that those external assets may already be tasked to other competing IRs and his needs will go unmet. Various tasking documents levy IRs on collection resources. Some tasking mechanisms are theater- or intelligence systems-unique. The Joint Tactical Exploitation of National Systems and various DIAMs specify procedures and formats for requesting support from national systems or agencies. Combatant commands will also modify, clarify or add to these procedures in their local intelligence SOPs or TTP.

Tasking Subordinate Elements

Recommending collection tasking to subordinate elements can be a lucrative source for satisfying IRs. Even Marines not assigned to an intelligence collection unit can provide valuable information, especially when in contact.

Often times at units below the MEF CE level-particularly at the battalion or squadron level-these taskings take the form of reconnaissance and surveillance (R&S) plans.

A mission tasking order goes to the unit selected to accomplish a particular collection mission. The selected unit makes the final determination of specific platforms, schedules, equipment, and personnel to be employed.

MAGTF Collection Tasking

There are many ways to task collection assets. The primary means to task MAGTF collection assets include the following:

- OPLAN/OPORD Intelligence Annex. Annex B, Intelligence, of the OPLAN/OPORD is the most commonly used vehicle for initial collection taskings. Appendix 10, Intelligence Operation Plan, contains the intelligence collection plan (appendix 10, Tab A).
- OPORD/FRAGO Execution Paragraph. Another tool for disseminating collection taskings is to include those taskings in paragraph 3 of the unit's warning, fragmentary or OPORD or in a stand-alone collection unit FRAGO. Detailed coordination must be conducted with the G-3/S-3 for this technique to succeed. Amplifying or supporting details can be included in annex B or its appendices as required.
- RFI. RFIs are any specific, time-sensitive IRs to support ongoing operations. It is not necessarily related to standing collection requirements or scheduled intelligence production. An RFI is initiated to respond to tactical requirements (critical information gaps and is validated in accordance with the unit's SOPs); e.g., a regimental S-2 may submit a time-sensitive RFI requesting confirmation of the size and composition of an enemy formation (no further information) reported by one of its battalions at a specific location. This would then be researched by higher headquarters G-2 staff and answered immediately if the information or intelligence exists. If the information or intelligence does not exist, the RFI would form the basis for an ICR that may result in a request for UAV support.

- Collection Emphasis Message. A collection emphasis message is another tool to broadly disseminate the MAGTF's collection focus. It is disseminated to higher, lower, and adjacent units; intelligence collectors; and intelligence exploitation and processing centers. It details the unit's PIR's and associated SIRs and SORs. The primary benefit of communicating collection intent is the operational perspective it provides organizations that may otherwise be isolated from the planning process. An informed collector can often amplify reporting to provide an answer that goes beyond immediate questions. See appendix E for a sample message.
- Statement of Intelligence Interest. A statement of intelligence interest (SII) is a comprehensive listing of a unit's IRs for a specified time period. The SII usually addresses long periods of time (2 to 3 years) and identifies broad areas of interest rather than specific information requirements addressed by SORs. All commands larger than battalions/squadrons should submit an SII and update it periodically. These SIIs are used to develop dissemination requirements for the DODIPP. The dissemination scheme may result in hardcopy or softcopy dissemination to units.

Exploitation and Reporting

Exploitation of collected information and reporting is closely associated with the management of collection assets and resources. Generally, the staff allocated a collection capability also controls the supporting processing, exploitation, analysis, and production response. The collection manager shares a responsibility for evaluating the collected information. The consumer—the supported commander or his users of intelligence—ultimately determines how well the IRs have been satisfied.

Techniques that assist in effective exploitations include cueing, redundancy, mix, integration, and coordination.

Cueing

Cueing uses one or more intelligence or reconnaissance asset to provide data directing collection by other intelligence or reconnaissance elements. Cueing maximizes the efficient use of finite collection assets in support of multiple, often competing, intelligence collection priorities.

Collection managers should plan to create opportunities for cued collection as part of the collection strategy; e.g., a HUMINT source may be employed 24 hours before a UAV mission to confirm or deny activity along a key corridor. If the HUMINT source reports the absence of activity, the UAV mission can be redirected to another area or used to confirm the absence of activity, depending on the relative priority of IRs. If the HUMINT source reports significant activity earlier than anticipated, the UAV mission may be accelerated to collect supporting detail, or instead retasked to another mission.

Cueing may occur dynamically (outside the collection strategy) as one intelligence or reconnaissance collector tips off another collector to a collection opportunity. Intelligence collection systems can drive operational tasking. This is most common when collection on a particular NAI triggers a decision corresponding to a decision point or fires at a target area of interest. Examples follow:

- An aviation ground attack mission is "tipped off" to specific threat air defense activity and flies a different ingress-egress profile.

- Indirect artillery fires are "cued" to more precise target areas.
- Ground maneuver elements are "tipped off" to changes in an expected enemy COA.

These examples illustrate the need for coordinating intelligence with other operations and demand the collection manager's active participation in the wargaming process when requirements are initially developed, and for close coordination with current operational intelligence, operations, and fires elements.

Redundancy

Redundancy planning is part of a collection strategy using several same-discipline assets to cover the same target. Redundancy is often used on high priority targets when the probability of any one intelligence or reconnaissance element adequately collecting is low. The probability of detection increases as a function of the number of collectors; e.g., if several SIGINT collectors focus on a designated emitter at different times, the probability of intercept improves, even if the emitter operates intermittently. The chance of acquiring accurate geolocational information using direction finding equipment is also improved through redundant collection tasking.

Mix

Mix means planning for complementary coverage by a combination of assets from multiple disciplines. Intelligence and reconnaissance mix techniques increase the probability of collection, reduce the risk of successful enemy deception, can facilitate cueing, and provide more complete intelligence reporting. The best mix of collectors puts the enemy in a dilemma. No matter what the enemy does (stays still or moves out), he is detected, identified, and possibly located; e.g., reconnaissance reports resupply activity within a known assembly area; SIGINT intercept of the associated logistics net provides unit identity, subordination, and indications of future activity.

Integration

Integration is the resource management aspect of collection strategy development. It involves integrating new requirements into planned or ongoing missions. Barring a decision to use redundant coverage for a critical target, collection managers must integrate new missions with previous planned or ongoing missions. Integration helps to avoid undertasking capable collectors. Resource integration examples are:

- Adding ICRs to a light armored reconnaissance battalion performing a zone reconnaissance mission.
- Inserting a new ICR during a preplanned UAV mission or replacing an existing requirement with one of higher priority.

Coordination

The collection manager must ensure the plan is coordinated. The collection manager develops SIR sets from the consolidated, validated, and prioritized list of PIRs and IRs. SIRs complete the collection strategy by associating each requirement with the corresponding decisions and time lines. Starting at the point that the commander requires intelligence to support a decision, the collection manager backward plans the collection mission to account for mission preparation, collection, reporting, processing, analysis, production, and dissemination.

One tool to coordinate the collection strategy with the planned friendly and estimated enemy operations is the intelligence synchronization matrix. In addition to the LTIOV determined by the prioritized IRs and associated decision and reporting criteria, the matrix records NAIs from the event template and reflects timelines of expected enemy activity from the IPB event template and the event matrix. The intelligence synchronization matrix provides the basic structure for the more detailed collection plan. See figure 3-1.

Report Formats

Standardized report formats support common understanding, interoperability, and efficient dissemination of collection results and other intelligence products. Standardized formats simplify and speed along the accurate, timely flow of reports from information collectors to intelligence analysts and allow their rapid incorporation via information systems into databases. Some of the more common reports used in collection reporting follow.

SIGINT

Most SIGINT reports are formatted and classified. Common reports include:

- SIGINT spot.
- SIGINT summary.
- Tactical.
- Tactical electronic intelligence.
- Critical intelligence.

These reports disseminate time-sensitive SIGINT information from collectors to requesters or intelligence consumers. However, information may also be disseminated using noncodeword reports. Unlike standard SIGINT product reports, noncodeword reports may be passed directly to commanders to allow immediate tactical use. Specific procedures for noncodeword reporting during operations should be in the SIGINT appendix to annex B of the OPORD. See MCWP 2-15.2.

Ground Reconnaissance

Reconnaissance teams report to their higher echelon of command. These reports are received in the SARC. The SARC also establishes priority reporting criteria for each committed team based on that team's information requirements. Normally, teams do not maintain constant radio communication while moving and sometimes while in observation posts, but they do monitor and transmit messages during the established windows.

TIME	T + 10	T + 24	T + 36	T + 48
Friendly Event	Penetrate 80th Corps	Shape 90th Corps	Shape 90th Corps	Shape reserve
Threat Event		Reserve departs assembly areas	Reserve deploys combat formation	Corps artillery forward deploys
Decision Points	Shift main effort to aviation combat element		Shift shaping actions	
Intelligence Event (PIR)	NAI 24-will the reserve reinforce 90th Corps	NAI 1-identify reserve assembly areas	NAI 3-identify reserve locations	NAI 3-identify Corps artillery refueler locations
Intelligence and Recon Collectors	JSTARS / Force Recon / UAV/ATARS / Ground Sensors	JSTARS	Force Recon / UAV/ATARS	JSTARS / Force Recon

Radio Battalion (spans T+10 through T+48)

Figure 3-1. Notional Intelligence Synchronization Matrix.

The SARC, however, establishes around-the-clock radio watches over primary and alternate nets so that teams can communicate immediately if necessary. Reporting windows may be established for the transmission of routine traffic or routine reports, such as situation reports. Other primary reconnaissance reports include:

- Size.
- Activity.
- Location.
- Unit.
- Time.
- Equipment.
- Hydrographic.
- Beach survey.
- Confirmatory beach.

- Surf.
- Landing zone.
- Road and route.
- Bridge.
- River/estuary.

See also MCRP 2-15.3B, *Reconnaissance Reports Guide.*

Measurement and SIGINT

Sensor information is like any intelligence information. It is analyzed and combined with other intelligence information to build a complete picture of the AO and the threat. The sensor report is the standard format used to report sensor data. This format is used for voice, data, and hardcopy reports. The general state of the sensor network, changes in the status of specific strings and relays, and planned sensor operations can be reported using the sensor status report. See MCWP 2-15.1.

Interrogator/Translator Operations

Results of interrogation of enemy prisoners of war and detainees provide a valuable source of intelligence information. The tactical interrogation report may provide a written summary of initial or subsequent interrogations. The document translation report may disseminate information resulting from captured enemy document exploitation. The intelligence information report format may also disseminate information derived from interrogation or translation. A HUMINT appendix may be included within Annex B, Intelligence, of the OPLAN/OPORD to establish standardized reporting procedures.

CI

CI assists in accomplishing three major objectives:

- Screening out refugees whose very presence threatens overall security of the force.
- Detecting enemy agents' intent on espionage, sabotage, terrorist or subversive missions against the force.
- Collecting information of value to other intelligence and security agencies.

The principal reports are the CI spot report, CI information report, and CI interrogation report. The CI spot report is a quick response report to get information into the all-source correlated database. The CI information report is a standard report used to report tactical CI information. The interrogation report is used to report interrogation information. MCWP 2-14 contains formats and specific instructions for completing these reports.

IMINT

IMINT mission results are reported in various reports. The specific type of report used is driven by the requirement originator's timeliness/currency concerns; i.e., LTIOV, and the type of mission being reported. All imagery reports are submitted via data or hardcopy format from the processing or exploitation center to the supported unit. IMINT reports are disseminated to adjacent and higher units. The reconnaissance exploitation report expeditiously reports results of an aerial imagery mission. Results should be disseminated within 1 hour of receipt of the imagery at the processing facility and focus exclusively on immediate information requirements. The initial photo interpretation report provides information on imagery collection missions not previously reported and can follow up any issued reconnaissance exploitation report with amplifying details. The supplemental photo interpretation report provides information not previously included in a reconnaissance exploitation report or initial photo interpretation report. See DIAM 57-05, *DOD Exploitation of Multi-Sensor Imagery*, and MCWP 2-15.4.

Miscellaneous Reports

- Response to RFI.
- Patrol.
- Mission.
- Ground reconnaissance or aircrew debriefing.
- Spot.
- Bombing, shelling, and mortaring location report.

The response to RFI report is generally submitted via data or hardcopy formats. The ground reconnaissance and aircrew debriefs are usually submitted via voice, however, aircrew debriefs are often submitted via message as mission reports. The bombing, shelling, and mortaring location report contains observance of enemy indirect fire weapons. This report is submitted via voice communications.

Supervision of the Collection Effort

Direction of the collection effort does not end with issuing SORs. The collection effort is continually supervised by the collection manager and coordinated with the C2 elements of the collection asset or resources. The focus is to ensure that collection agencies have received SORs and that they are clearly understood. Coordination is conducted with processing and exploitation centers and among MAGTF collection operations officers and those of higher, adjacent, and subordinate units.

Functions

Monitoring

Monitoring of ongoing collection operations is conducted to ensure that PIRs and other IRs are being satisfied and that they are done so in a timely manner. Intelligence reports received are reconciled with the requested LTIOV of requirements to assess the timeliness and responsiveness of the collection operations. Monitoring is conducted by the requester, the collection manager, and the production and exploitation centers.

Evaluating

The evaluation process tracks the status of collection requirements and provides feedback to the requesters. When collection results are provided, the collection manager evaluates the reports for the following:

- Completeness.
- Clarity.
- Adherence to specified reporting criteria.
- Responsiveness to users' intelligence and timeliness satisfaction.

- Identification of opportunities to cue other intelligence and reconnaissance collection resources.

Requester feedback establishes customer satisfaction, permits tasker deletion, and frees collection assets and resources to be redirected to satisfy other active requirements.

Updating

Based on the requester's assessment of requirement satisfaction, the collection manager reviews priorities for currency. The collection plan is updated to include retasking (if the requirement is not satisfied), adding new requirements based on the impact of changes in planned friendly operations, changes in known or assessed enemy operations or canceling satisfied requirements. It is imperative that the collection plan be continually updated and those changes communicated to higher, lower, and adjacent units to maximize collection operations efficiencies.

Duties

Collection Manager

The collection manager should prioritize IRs, convert them into collection requirements, and coordinate actions with appropriate collections agencies. The collection manager must continually seek to maximize the effectiveness of limited collection resources within operational time constraints.

P&A Cell OIC

Primary responsibility is to manage and supervise the MAGTFs all-source intelligence processing and production efforts.

SARC OIC

As one of the focal points for intelligence reporting from organic assets, the SARC OIC must screen the intelligence reporting and interface with intelligence analysts to see if reporting is satisfying stated requirements.

Subordinate Unit Intelligence Officers

Supervisory responsibilities at the tactical level include ensuring that IRs are correctly prioritized and submitted and that feedback in the form of an evaluation is provided to the collection manager and/or collectors. This two-way communication enables requestors to clarify issues that may not be understood by collectors.

Updating the Collection Plan During Execution

As information is reported from collectors and new IRs are generated throughout the MAGTF, IRs and the collection plan require updating. If the data is insufficient, additional collection may be coordinated with the collection manager. At this point, the processed requirement transitions out of the COM cycle. The collection manager and the P&A cell OIC, in coordination with the SARC OIC and requesters, continually assess the effectiveness of collection operations and how quality and timeliness may be improved. As the collection plan is updated, all subordinate commanders and their intelligence officers must be informed so they may be apprised of ongoing MAGTF intelligence collection operations. Direct communication with those directly affected is critical. Broad dissemination of intelligence collection plan updates may be accomplished by web-based or other automated means.

CHAPTER 4
PLANNING AND EXECUTION

The intelligence collection effort must support and adapt to the MAGTF commander's intent, concepts of intelligence and operations, and the supporting scheme of maneuver. Key questions for operational integration include the following:

- What is the MAGTF AO and the area of interest?
- What is the MAGTF concept of operations, task organization, and main and supporting efforts?
- What are the standing PIRs and IRs? Which have been tasked to supporting units? What specific information is the commander most interested in; i.e., enemy ground operations, enemy air operations, target BDA, friendly force protection or enemy future intentions?
- What is the concept of MAGTF fires support? How will MAGTF target development and target intelligence be conducted? What are the specific collection needs to support these?
- What are the concepts of intelligence and operations of other JTF, component, and theater resources? What are the task organization and command/support relationships for all MAGTF intelligence and reconnaissance units?
- How can naval collection assets and other Services, JTF, theater, and national collection assets be employed and integrated to support MAGTF operations?

Terrain

Terrain factors have a significant impact on intelligence collection operations, particularly on the ability of certain sensors to "see" through vegetation; requirements for line of sight communications; and employment considerations in intelligence collection operations and for the time-sensitive dissemination of collected intelligence products by MAGTF CIS. Many intelligence collection systems require line of sight with the target area to be effective. Accordingly, collection planners must assess the effects of mountains, defilade, vegetation, and other potential terrain obstacles on planned collection operations.

Weather

Weather is a key limiting factor in some collection operations. Bad weather may degrade identifying and locating targets. Weather can also limit the type of collection capabilities that may be employed. Low ceilings and poor visibility can decrease visual reconnaissance effectiveness and the resolution of photographic systems.

Threat

Detailed threat analysis must be conducted to determine the intelligence collection sensors and platforms that can be employed effectively against a given enemy and how to employ limited MAGTF and external resources to obtain the best possible intelligence. Collection operations can be hampered by the enemy's air defense capability and his camouflage, cover, concealment, and deception activities. Threat EW capabilities must be determined to assess their effects on UAVs, manned platforms radio uplink, and various downlinks.

Coordination with Maneuver and Fires

Maneuver and fires considerations include many issues requiring precoordination and several organizations and command echelons needed for the coordination. The detailed procedures needed to execute maneuver and fires to collection and integration of collection operations into the MAGTF maneuver and fires scheme should be included in unit SOPs. Main operational issues follow:

- Requests and coordination of air support and integration within the air tasking order.
- Fires planning and necessary fire control measures (restricted fire areas and no fire areas).
- Necessary maneuver control measures (insertion and extraction requirements and plans to include short-notice emergency extractions).
- Collectors operating within subordinate unit AO under a wide range of command relationships.
- Collection missions being tasked to nonprimary intelligence collectors; i.e., infantry battalions, combat engineers, and pilots.
- Emergency action planning, to include escape and evasion planning.
- Other tasks to be performed or supported by other MAGTF units; e.g., sensor inserts.
- Integrating collectors within landing and other movement plans.
- Coordination, deconfliction, and management of UAV operations with other MAGTF air operations.

Communications and Information Systems

Whether communications are analog or digital, voice or data, secure or nonsecure, there are hosts of technical details to be addressed in the planning stages to ensure collection activities succeed. Key CIS requirements and planning considerations to support MAGTF collection operations follow:

- Ensure that the MAGTF CE G-2/S-2, intelligence battalion, intelligence collection elements, and other MAGTF units are included in the distribution of intelligence-related address indicator groups to receive pertinent JTF, theater, and national intelligence and CI products.

- Determine and coordinate radio nets requirements, supporting frequencies, and operational procedures; e.g., external to MAGTF, internal MAGTF, intelligence broadcasts, retransmission sites, routine and time-sensitive operations.
- Coordination of CIS activation and restoration priorities and supporting procedures.
- Communications security material system requirements for unique collection-related communications and related security material.
- Determine and coordinate wire communications, including telephones.
- Establish, operate, and manage unique collection communications.
- Determine and coordinate local and wide area networks and unique intelligence networks information systems requirements; e.g., hardware, software, Internet protocol addresses.
- Integrate collection element CIS operations with those of other MAGTF and pertinent JTF and other components intelligence and reconnaissance units; e.g., mutual support, cueing.
- Communications integration of collection elements employed in general support (GS) with other MAGTF elements; e.g., to provide time-sensitive reporting, coordination of maneuver.
- Coordination of collection CIS and dissemination operations and procedures with allied and coalition forces.
- Manual dissemination procedures; e.g., courier must be established and practiced.

Combat Service Support Availability

Logistical considerations affecting collection operations include the following:

- Batteries and other power requirements.
- Transportation.
- Water.
- Food.
- Ammunition.
- Integration of collector's embarkation and load plans into those of the supported unit.

Employment of MAGTF Intelligence Units

MAGTF intelligence units are employed to meet the requirements of the entire force. The MAGTF G-2/S-2 develops a concept of intelligence support, which employs these units on the basis of the MAGTF mission, PIRs, concept of operations, and commander's intent. This concept must integrate intelligence activities with operations to provide key intelligence to commanders to enable rapid and effective decisionmaking. Based on the results of IPB analysis and the concept of operations, assets are positioned to—

- Satisfy PIRs.
- Expose enemy vulnerabilities.
- Monitor key locations.
- Detect and assist in the engagement of targets.
- Identify opportunities as they arise in the battlespace.

Intelligence units are employed in GS or DS. Under GS, units are tasked by the MAGTF commander through his G-2/S-2 to satisfy the requirements of the entire force. Because of the limited number of specialized intelligence assets and their ability to develop intelligence that is relevant to current and future operations in all areas of the battlespace (deep, close, and rear), GS is the preferred support relationship. Under DS, the requirements of a supported commander are given priority. DS is used to focus intelligence support for particular phases of an operation or create enhanced intelligence nodes to support MAGTF subordinate elements. When MAGTFs smaller than a full MEF are deployed, they will normally be supported by attached, task-organized detachments from the intelligence battalion, the force reconnaissance company, and the radio battalion.

Focused Intelligence Support

Intelligence must be integrated with the mission, commander's intent, and concept of operations and should normally be weighted to support the main effort. The MAGTF intelligence structure has the flexibility to tailor its capabilities to meet the requirements of various types of expeditionary operations, and adapt to changing operational needs during execution. For each operation, the MAGTF G-2/S-2 will assess IRs and develop a concept of intelligence support that positions assets where they can best satisfy those requirements. Intelligence nodes will focus support within the MAGTF. Split-basing will build intelligence nodes within and outside the AO to deliver comprehensive and reliable intelligence support while reducing the size of the deployed force. Intelligence units and DS teams are employed to tailor and enhance the capabilities of organic intelligence sections or to create task-organized intelligence nodes in response to specific requirements.

Task Organization of Intelligence Support Units

Task organization of intelligence support units is one of the principal means for the MAGTF commander to shape the intelligence effort. Collection, exploitation, and unique production capabilities of specialized intelligence units significantly enhance the ability of supported G-2/S-2 sections to develop timely, mission-focused intelligence. Intelligence battalion, force reconnaissance company, and radio battalion elements task-organize to provide tailored intelligence capabilities. Specific capabilities provided are based on the threat, the supported unit's anticipated requirements (as determined through IPB), and the concept of operations.

Elements from some or all of the intelligence battalion's subordinate companies combine into intelligence battalion detachments. The CI/HUMINT company provides HUMINT exploitation teams (HETs). The radio battalion forms task-organized SIGINT support units (SSUs), which provide a mix of SIGINT and EW capabilities. When MAGTFs smaller than a full MEF deploy, an intelligence battalion detachment, a HET, force reconnaissance platoons, and a radio battalion SSU will normally be attached to the MAGTF CE. In MEF operations, when the entire radio battalion, intelligence battalion, and force reconnaissance company are employed, detachments, HETs, SSUs, and platoons may be placed in DS as required. Those subordinate units provide tailored intelligence capabilities to create an enhanced intelligence node to support an MSC or other MAGTF element.

Intelligence Direct Support Teams

Intelligence DS teams are organic to the intelligence battalion and each of the division, Marine aircraft wing (MAW), and force service support group G-2/S-2 sections. Teams are made up of one officer and several enlisted personnel who have a mix of intelligence specialty skills. DS teams provide an enhanced analytical and dissemination capability to a unit intelligence section and link the intelligence structure to the supported units. As assigned by the G-2/S-2, they augment the supported unit's intelligence section to carry out the following tasks:

- Perform analysis and production to support future operations.
- Tailor all-source fusion center and other external source intelligence products to the needs of the supported commander.

- Assist in the management of external intelligence support requirements.
- Facilitate dissemination of intelligence received from external sources.

The MEF and MSC G-2/S-2s use their DS teams to tailor and focus intelligence support to units designated as the main effort or to create enhanced intelligence nodes at key times and places in the battlespace. See MCWP 2-1.

Precrisis (Garrison/Peacetime) Intelligence Collection

The predominant collection focus during precrisis phases is obtaining basic or encyclopedic intelligence on the AO and current intelligence on the threat. In researching current or basic intelligence, intelligence analysts will consult various databases or online sources. National and theater resources are relied on heavily.

The Planning Phase

The planning phase is a critical phase where the foundation of intelligence preparation is set for the duration of the operation. There is an enormous demand for intelligence information and pressure to produce a high volume of intelligence in a very short time. The paradox is that although requirements will be very high, intelligence personnel are constrained by a lack of physical ability to collect before actual contact and a short time span to produce results. The lack of time is complicated by a need to prepare the intelligence collection section and units to conduct predeployment activities. Reliance on national and theater intelligence resources is still the predominant theme. The primary focus of collection is on basic or encyclopedic intelligence if this was not adequately done during the precrisis phase; otherwise the collection effort is concentrated more on supporting current and estimative intelligence in support of operational planning. During planning, intelligence focuses on describing the battlespace through IPB and satisfying the commander's critical IRs and related PIRs. See MCWP 5-1, *Marine Corps Planning Process.*

Intelligence Collection During Execution

Intelligence collection during execution differs significantly from intelligence collection during planning.

Intelligence collection support during the precrisis or warning phases requires developing a large volume of basic intelligence and preparation of broad-scope estimates needed to develop and analyze COAs. However, *intelligence collection support during the execution phase must try to satisfy a much larger body of IRs in a significantly greater degree of detail.* For example, the nature of the intelligence required by a MAGTF commander to decide if a noncombatant evacuation operation is feasible differs radically from the type and detail of intelligence required by the mission commander who will execute the operation.

Another major difference is the time available to satisfy IRs. In the *execution phase there is a significant increase of time-sensitive IRs. Intelligence must often be developed in hours, minutes or even seconds.* Success often depends on the ability to provide immediate answers to critical questions regarding threat force dispositions and intentions.

Once the execution phase begins, the clash of opposing forces normally causes significant changes in the situation. *The changing nature of requirements accelerates.* Predicting enemy capabilities and intentions becomes increasingly difficult once the execution phase begins, but it is specifically during this period that the commander requires detailed and accurate intelligence to reduce uncertainty.

National and theater resources continue to be employed but a greater reliance may be placed on organic assets, particularly those in support of forward-deployed forces. Collection planning remains centralized but may be decentralized once a main effort is established and assets are attached to or placed to support the main effort.

The combined factors of the wide-ranging nature of IRs, the degree of detail required, the limited time available, and the uncertainty inherent during execution combine to make collection support to execution the most significant intelligence challenge. Collection managers must be prepared to meet this challenge and provide the flexibility required to deliver continuous situational awareness, identify opportunities, and facilitate rapid decisionmaking during execution.

Current Operations

The collection support effort during current operations consists primarily of answering previously developed intelligence reporting criteria and emerging requirements that arise as opposing forces clash. Coordination of ongoing and planned collection operations with other intelligence collectors and all current operation centers or battlefield agencies is emphasized. Factors critical to ensuring timely and effective dissemination are established and intelligence reporting criteria are widely disseminated. Each intelligence collector or the reporting unit; i.e., SARC or reconnaissance operations center, must be able to evaluate and assess the relevance of information to the ongoing operations. Each piece of collected data must undergo an immediate tactical processing and assessment before dissemination. A keen situational awareness and understanding of the unit's OPLAN/OPORD is required by all intelligence personnel, including collection managers and SARC personnel. Support must include intelligence collection to support deep and rear operations, resisting the natural tendency to focus on the close battle. Support to current operations must be balanced against the requirement to support future operations. All assets cannot be devoted to current operations at the expense of supporting planning for future operations.

Future Operations

Intelligence collection support to future operations represents only a small portion of the collection effort, but merits discussion. Support is influenced by the timeframe and scope of the operation, level of command, identification of PIRs, and availability of collectors. One collection strategy discussed earlier endorsed "fencing of collection assets." One of the primary contributions of intelligence collection support to future operations is support to BDA that inputs to combat assessment, which in turn helps determine the nature of future operations. The collection operations officer's role is crucial. Continuous interaction by the collection operations officer and the intelligence plans officer in the future operations cell and the MAGTF P&A cell OIC is key to focusing intelligence collection efforts to support future operations. As decisions are made, ICRs and priorities for specific collection missions and tasks are generated and assessed against previously identified requirements.

APPENDIX A
SAMPLE INTELLIGENCE REQUIREMENTS WORKSHEET

MEF IR Number (1)	Requester IR Number (2)	DTG Received (3)	Subject (4)	Action (5)	Status (6)
04-1012	1st Marine Division Number 04-001	090830 Jan	Reconnaissance activity in NAI 32	SOR Numbers 04-1462 (UAV) 04-1463 (GSP) 04-1464 (Force Reconnaissance)	
04-1013	MEF Engineer	090900 Jan	Obstacle system at Objective SCHMIDT	For situation template	Closed 091630 Jan
04-1014	MEF G-2/P&A Cell	101100 Jan	Imagery of landing beaches	Forwarded to JTF J-2 for national collection	Pending

Column 1: The MEF IR number for ease of tracking.

Column 2: The originating requester IR number is posted to correlate subordinate requirements with the MAGTF. If the requirement is generated by the MAGTF CE, list that office. *Note: for requirements that are forwarded to higher headquarters, no notation is made.*

Column 3: When the information requirement is received.

Column 4: A succinct description indicating the information requirement subject.

Column 5: What SORs are germane to this requirement. *Note: one example identifies the collection system tasked to satisfy each SOR.*

Column 6: The information requirement is still active, pending or closed.

APPENDIX B
SAMPLE INTELLIGENCE COLLECTION WORKSHEET DESCRIPTION

Period Covered (From 21 Jan _____ to Seizure of Objective Schmidt)

Collection planning for a particular operation commences with the receipt or deduction of a mission by the commander and continues until the mission is accomplished. The collection worksheet covers the period from initiation of planning until accomplishment of the mission. However, in an amphibious operation, certain IRs may be directly related to various phases of the operation or must be satisfied as a prerequisite to other planning; e.g., IRs about location of suitable beaches or helicopter landing zones must be satisfied long before the actual assault. Therefore, the period entered at the top of the form may be less than that of the plan as a whole. The worksheet must be revised as IRs develop or no longer apply, as available collection agencies change in number and type, and as specific collection missions become obsolete. To accommodate the revisions, a collection worksheet should be maintained in loose leaf form.

Column 1, PIRs

Lists the IRs that must be satisfied. These include the PIRs and other IRs.

Column 2, Indicators

For each PIR and IR, the intelligence officer lists the indicators derived from an analysis of the enemy and the characteristics of the objective area or target indicator for each PIR/IR. Indications are positive or negative evidence. There usually is more than one indicator for each PIR/IR. When available, they will satisfy the particular requirement. Indications form the basis for developing SIRs and SORs for the collection of information.

Column 3, SIRs

Contains the specific information required; i.e., "the collectible info" that will substantiate or refute each indication listed in column 2.

Having determined what indications point to the solution of a particular IR, the intelligence officer next determines what information is needed to substantiate or refute each indication. For example, if removal of mines and obstacles is an indication of an enemy attack, then the SIR is if the enemy is actually removing mines and obstacles.

Reluctance of prisoners to remain in forward areas may be an indication of enemy preparations to employ nuclear weapons. The SIR is whether or not prisoners demonstrate any marked eagerness to be evacuated from the combat area.

Improvement of enemy positions may be an indication of defense. The SIR is if the enemy is actually improving his positions.

Information to be sought then becomes the basis for SORs for collection of information. A collection agency in most cases is not assigned full responsibility for establishing that any particular indication exists.

For example, increased patrolling may be an indication that an enemy is preparing to attack. A rifle company would not be asked if there was an increase in enemy patrol activity in its sector. Instead, the specific information to be sought that forms the basis for an order to the company would be to report the frequency of enemy patrols encountered in its sector.

Another indication of attack might be forward echeloning of artillery. The specific information to be sought by a collection agency is not if artillery is being echeloned forward but to report the location of artillery in certain forward areas.

In the above two examples, the intelligence officer is the one in the best position to make proper deductions. From the information he receives and after comparison with information already available, the intelligence officer can deduce if there has been an increase in enemy patrolling, and if the enemy artillery is being echeloned forward to support the attack.

The intelligence officer carefully studies the AO and the known enemy situation to focus the collection effort on a specific area; e.g., in developing specific information to be sought on possible enemy reinforcement, the intelligence officer studies the road nets and suitable avenues of approach to determine logical routes that enemy reinforcements would move. The specific information to be sought then becomes the volume and type of traffic along a particular road or in a particular area. The intelligence officer then has a basis for developing plans for aerial reconnaissance or establishing observation posts.

Column 4, Agencies to be Employed

List all currently available agencies. The list includes not only subordinate units but also higher and adjacent commands that gather information of value. In addition to troop units, the list of agencies includes intelligence specialists such as CI, imagery interpretation, and interrogation-translator personnel. The listing of troop units is not restricted to combat elements.

Following his determination of the specific information to be sought, the intelligence officer selects the collection agencies that will be tasked to furnish information. In making his selections, he is guided by considerations of capability, suitability, multiplicity, and balance.

Orders and RFIs are issued only to those agencies that are physically capable of providing it in time of use. The intelligence officer must be cognizant of the location, status, and current and projected missions of all available agencies.

Agencies selected to gather information are those best suited for the task; e.g., a trained force reconnaissance unit is normally better suited for amphibious reconnaissance than a patrol from a rifle company. An information collection mission is consistent with the tactical or logistics officer. Suitability also includes consideration of economy of force. Before an agency is selected for a particular task, the intelligence officer considers what other collection tasks the agency might accomplish simultaneously.

Information is evaluated and interpreted to derive intelligence. Accurate evaluation requires comparison of information obtained from several sources and agencies. Whenever possible, the intelligence officer selects more than one agency to collect information (redundancy).

Finally, the intelligence officer endeavors to balance the collection workload among available agencies. Although desirable, balance is the least important consideration in the selection of agencies, and more often, careful consideration of capabilities and suitability results in adequate distribution of the workload.

Column 5, Place and Time to Report

Reflects the place and time that information is to be reported. Information that arrives too late is of no value. The intelligence officer must effectively meet the needs of the commander, other staff officers, and higher, adjacent, and subordinate units.

- Be specific, especially for electronic reporting. When reporting via automated information and communications systems, a requester should be very specific; e.g., if an actual image is requested, how should it be disseminated? Posted on a classified web page? Posted on an imagery dissemination server? If so, which one? If an electronic file transfer is desired, what is the Internet protocol address and circuit the requester uses? Any special report formatting requirements should be included if a non-standard product is requested.

- One-time versus periodic reporting. For reconnaissance missions, one-time reporting may be sufficient. For surveillance missions, periodic reporting is usually required. Requirements supporting target or area surveillance should have details on how frequently reports are to be generated.

- Include LTIOV. The LTIOV is an appropriate entry in the reporting column. Entries may specify an exact time for reporting and/or not-later-than times for periodic reports (or at such times that information is obtained). Negative reports, if desired, are also indicated.

- Routine vs time-sensitive. Clearly identify criteria and reporting channels for routine and time-sensitive reports.

Column 6, Remarks

Miscellaneous remarks on the progress of the collection are recorded in column 6 of the worksheet. The intelligence officer develops a simple code to indicate PIRs/IRs that require revision or cancellation. Prompt cancellation of orders and requests for collection of information, including PIRs, is mandatory if the efforts of collection agencies are to be focused properly. A unit SOP for intelligence functioning normally provides for routine reporting of certain types of information. A note is made in the collection worksheet when certain information requirements are covered by the SOPs; e.g., the reporting of minefields may be prescribed by the unit SOP. A requirement for information on the enemy's use of mines can be handled by placing "SOP" in column 6, and responsibility need not be indicated under agencies. However, a requirement for reporting the location of minefields in the vicinity of a specific area is not treated as an SOP item. Finally, the intelligence officer notes those specific information requirements that can be combined into a single order of request to an agency.

PIRs	Indicators	SIRs	DIV	MAW	FSSG	CI/HUMINT	VMU	RadBn	VMAQ	Force Recon	GSP	Place and Time to Report	Remarks
						Agencies to be Employed							
Will the 3d Tank Division enter NAI 8 or 9 on the evening of 22 January?	Dispersal of tanks and self-propelled artillery to forward positions.	Will more than 220 combat vehicles of 3d Tank Division pass through NAI 8 or 9 between 221600 and 230400 January? Will more than 38 artillery weapons subordinate to 3d Tank Division enter NAI 8 or 9 between 221600 and 230400 January?	X	X	X	X	X			X	X	Report by fastest means to MEF G-2 LTIOV: 230400 January	
	Increased communications by 3d Tank Division elements.	Are enemy tactical radios active in NAI 8 or 9 before 230400 January?	X	X	X			X	X			Report by fastest means to MEF G-2 LTIOV: 230400 January	

Figure B-1. Sample Intelligence Collection Worksheet.

APPENDIX C
SAMPLE INTELLIGENCE COLLECTION PLAN

CLASSIFICATION

Copy no.___ of___ copies
Headquarters, (MAGTF)
PLACE OF ISSUE
Date/time group
Message reference number

TAB A (Intelligence Collection Plan) TO APPENDIX 10 (Intelligence OPLAN) TO ANNEX B (Intelligence) TO OPLAN

(U) REFERENCES:

   (a) Theater TTP
   (b) MEF Tactical SOP
   (c) MCWP 2-1

1. (U) <u>Situation</u>. Remaining Orange Force is defending against the Blue Force's advance to prevent the destruction of the ruling regime in the capital city of Orangeville. They intend to delay and attrite Blue Force to such an extent that US resolve to continue the war will fail, allowing the Orange regime to survive through diplomatic means.

   (a) (U) See FRAGO.
   (b) (U) Enemy situation.
   (c) (U) Most dangerous COA.
   (d) (U) Most likely COA.

2. (U) <u>Mission</u>. To provide R&S of MEF battlespace to support Blue Force attacks in zone, confirm conditions for amphibious landing, and determine status of Orange Force's location.

3. (U) <u>Execution</u>

   a. (U) National and theater collection will be requested to support MEF deep IRs (beyond forward boundary/deep battle synchronization line), threats to MEF flanks and logistic support bases, and against threats within MEF's boundaries beyond organic collection capabilities. Of particular in-

Page number

CLASSIFICATION

CLASSIFICATION

terest are enemy strategic and operational reserve forces that could influence MEF advance, and indications of Orange Force use of weapons of mass destruction.

(1) (U) In accordance with references (a) and (b), and as the Blue Force supporting effort during this operation, MEF battlespace R&S will rely heavily on organic aviation and battlefield surveillance/collection assets to satisfy IRs to support the close and deep fight.

(2) (U) Due to the location of the ground component commander to the flank and rear, and the commander, amphibious task force (CATF)/commander, landing force (CLF) relationship to execute an amphibious landing, MEF will request lateral intelligence reporting from the ground and naval component commanders. Lateral ground component commander intelligence reporting to MEF will facilitate cross-boundry operations and rear area operations/support requirements. Lateral naval component commanders intelligence reporting will support the movement of MEF's operating in littoral areas, and assist in determining enemy activity within the battlespace.

(3) (U) Upon chop of the CLF to MEF, selected R&S assets DS of CATF will become operational control to the MEF G-2.

(4) (U) Organic Focus. All organic R&S assets will focus on satisfying MEF PIRs/IRs. Ground-based SIGINT collection will focus on indications and warning force protection reporting to the supported commander. Forward CI and HUMINT assets will provide the supported commander with tactical interrogations and refugee debriefs; rear area CI assets will provide CI force protection source operations. MEF ground R&S operations will provide continuous observation and operate in vicinity of MEF NAIs and targeted areas of interest as directed. Visual aerial reconnaissance will provide timely battlespace awareness within the MEF AO, and support time-sensitive and ad hoc emerging IRs utilizing in-flight and post mission reporting. Ground sensor operations will be focused along major lines of communications (LOCs) and boundaries within and along the MEF area of responsibility. Organic MEF UAVs will be flown in GS of MEF operating forces. All collection disciplines will support personnel recovery operations as required.

b. (U) Concept Of Operations

(1) (U) The MEF R&S Plan will be divided in the following three stages:

- Stage A: Prechop of landing force.
- Stage B: Postchop of landing force.
- Stage C: Seizure of Orangeville.

Page number

CLASSIFICATION

CLASSIFICATION

(2) (U) <u>Stage A: Prechop of Landing Force</u>. During Stage A, R&S focus will be—

- Protection of our MEF units.
- Intentions of enemy forces able to influence MEF flanks, the amphibious landing zone or moving into adjacent units.
- Determining if conditions are met for MEF to assume operational control of landing force.
- Disposition of Orange Force's operational reserve forces that could move to impede MEF's movement.
- Status of LOCs.
- Disposition of enemy forces in the vicinity of Orangeville.

(3) (U) <u>Stage B: Postchop of Landing Force</u>. During Stage B, R&S focus will be—

- Disposition of Orange Force's operational reserves that could impede the MEF's movement or move into an adjacent unit's zone.
- Orange Force's operational reserves that could attack MEF's flanks.
- Status of LOCs from Badguyburg to Orangeville.
- Threats to MEF's rear area.
- Potential areas for interdiction west of Orangeville.

(4) (U) <u>Stage C: Seizure of Orangeville</u>. During Stage C, R&S focus will be—

- Disposition of enemy forces in the vicinity Orangeville.
- Enemy forces that can influence LOCs.
- Identification of enemy units able to attack Blue Force's flanks.
- Threats to Blue Force rear area.
- Potential areas for interdiction west of Orangeville.
- Suspected movement of Orange Force.

(5) (U) <u>Concept for SIGINT Collection</u>. MEF organic ground-based SIGINT collection assets are in GS of MEF and DS of the supported commander. Theater and national SIGINT collection will be requested as required.

(a) (U) <u>Communications Intelligence</u>. MEF organic ground-based communications intelligence collection will focus on indications, warning reporting, and force protection to the supported commander. Collection emphasis will be—

- Range Force's corps and C2 divisions.
- Artillery fire direction nets.
- Success of Blue Force's deception plan as to actual location of amphibious landing site.

Page number

CLASSIFICATION

CLASSIFICATION

(b) (U) <u>Electronic Intelligence</u>. Blue Force electronic intelligence surveillance support will focus on indications and warning reporting and force protection of Blue Force. Collection emphasis will be—

- PIR support.
- Locating remaining radar guided air defense weapons.
- Indications of possible air attacks within MEF AO.
- Indications of possible employment of weapons of mass destruction.

(6) (U) <u>Concept for CI/HUMINT Collection</u>. Forward CI/HUMINT assets will focus on—

- Force protection.
- Assisting in Blue Force deception plan as to actual location of amphibious landing site.
- Assisting in Blue Force deception plan to convince Orange Force national-level commanders that MEF is the Blue Force main effort.
- Conducting tactical interrogations to support the commander's PIRs/IRs. Rear area CI assets will provide CI force protection source operations. Postchop, selected CATF assets will become operational control to MEF and report and receive tasking from the MEF G-2.

(7) (U) <u>Concept for Ground R&S Collection</u>. MEF ground R&S operations will be conducted with—

- MSC ground reconnaissance assets having collection responsibility from forward line of troops to other phase lines in effect.
- MEF force reconnaissance assets (force reconnaissance companies and radio battalion radio reconnaissance teams) having collection responsibility from fire support coordination line to forward boundary/deep battle synchronization line.
- DS unconventional warfare forces having collection responsibility beyond the forward boundary/deep battle synchronization line. Cross-boundary ground R&S operations will be conducted by MEF vice MSC ground R&S assets. Postchop, selected CATF ground R&S assets will become operational control to MEF, and report and receive tasking from the Blue Force G-2.

(8) (U) <u>Concept for Aerial Visual R&S Collection</u>. MEF aerial visual R&S collection will center on the aviation assets of the MAW. Because of the dynamic reporting capability of aircraft operating within the Blue Force battlespace, aerial visual R&S will provide timely battlespace awareness, and support time-sensitive

Page number

CLASSIFICATION

CLASSIFICATION

and adhoc emerging IRs utilizing in-flight and post mission reporting. Time-critical ad hoc IRs will be forwarded to the tactical aircraft command center via the MEF air officer. When directed, positive and negative reporting is required in specific collection requirements or emphasis.

(9) (U) <u>Concept for Ground Sensor Collection</u>. MEF will provide GSP squads to ground maneuver commands in DS to facilitate close battle operations. GSP assets retained by the MEF collection management and dissemination officer will be focused along major LOCs and command boundaries within and along the MEF area of responsibility. Postchop, selected CATF ground sensor assets will become operational control to MEF, and report and receive tasking from the MEF G-2.

(10) (U) <u>Concept for UAV Collection</u>. Organic MEF UAV will be flown in DS and GS of MEF maneuver forces. Remote receive stations will be collocated with maneuver forces to allow rapid transfer of time-critical information. The aviation combat element commander will recommend possible forward base locations for future operations.

(11) (U) <u>Concept for Aerial Imagery Collection</u>. Requests for national and theater imagery collection will be forwarded to higher headquarters for satisfaction. Aerial imagery collection will support recurring IRs along LOCs or against point targets.

   c. (U) <u>Tasks</u>

      (1) (U) GCEs

         (a) (U) <u>1st Marine Division (MARDIV)</u>

<u>1</u> (U) Conduct organic R&S operations in zone to the intelligence handover line in effect.

<u>2</u> (U) Debrief all organic R&S teams providing intelligence reports to MEF G-2 operations within 6 hours.

<u>3</u> (U) Receive and incorporate one squad from the GSP in DS for R&S operations. Implanting of sensors is the responsibility of supported unit.

<u>4</u> (U) Assist in recovery of MEF and unconventional warfare R&S assets in zone.

<u>5</u> (U) Evacuate captured personnel and materiel from the forward collection point to the central collection point by most expeditious means possible. Enforce tagging procedures in accordance with reference (b). Interrogations will only be conducted by MEF HUMINT personnel.

Page number

CLASSIFICATION

CLASSIFICATION

<u>6</u> (U) Receive and incorporate one company (1st/2d) Radio Battalion (-) (Reinforced) in DS.

<u>7</u> (U) Receive remote receive station team from Marine unmanned aerial vehicle squadron (VMU)-1.

<u>8</u> (U) Receive CI/HUMINT elements in GS.

(b) (U) <u>2d MARDIV</u>

<u>1</u> (U) Conduct organic R&S operations in zone to the intelligence handover line in effect.

<u>2</u> (U) Debrief all organic R&S teams providing summary reports to MEF G-2 operations within 6 hours.

<u>3</u> (U) Assist in recovery of MEF and unconventional warfare R&S assets in zone.

<u>4</u> (U) Evacuate captured personnel and materiel from the forward collection point to the central collection point by most expeditious means possible. Enforce tagging procedures in accordance with reference (b). Interrogations will only be conducted by Blue Force HUMINT personnel.

<u>5</u> (U) Receive remote receive station team from VMU-1.

<u>6</u> (U) Receive and incorporate one squad from the ground sensor platoon in GS for R&S operations. Implanting of sensors is the responsibility of supported unit.

(c) (U) <u>3d MARDIV (Stages B and C)</u>

<u>1</u> (U) Maintain DS R&S units until notified otherwise by this HQ.

<u>2</u> (U) Conduct organic R&S operations in zone as directed.

<u>3</u> (U) Debrief all organic R&S teams providing intelligence reports to the MEF G-2 operations within 6 hours.

<u>4</u> (U) Assist in recovery of MEF and unconventional warfare R&S assets in zone.

<u>5</u> (U) Evacuate captured personnel and materiel from the forward collection point to the central collection point by most expeditious means possible. Enforce tagging procedures in accordance with reference (b). Interrogations will only be conducted by MEF HUMINT personnel.

<u>6</u> (U) Receive remote receive station team from VMU-1.

Page number

CLASSIFICATION

CLASSIFICATION

(d) (U) <u>4th MARDIV (Stages B and C)</u>

<u>1</u> (U) Conduct organic R&S operations in zone to established phase lines in effect.

<u>2</u> (U) Debrief all organic R&S teams providing summary reports to MEF G-2 operations within 6 hours.

<u>3</u> (U) Assist in recovery of MEF and unconventional warfare forces R&S assets in zone.

<u>4</u> (U) Evacuate captured personnel and materiel from the forward collection point to the central collection point most expeditious means possible. Enforce tagging procedures in accordance with reference (b). Interrogations will only be conducted by MEF HUMINT personnel.

<u>5</u> (U) Receive remote receive station team from VMU-1.

(2) (U) <u>MAW</u>

(a) (U) Provide timely intelligence reports as required to MEF G-2 operations officer.

(b) (U) Use strike camera to greatest extent possible to support first phase BDA.

(c) (U) Conduct UAV operations from Texaco forward arming and refueling point until a forward site for control can safely be established and maintained.

(d) (U) Provide two man operation planning/liaison team (UAV detachment) to MEF SARC.

(e) (U) Provide emergency extract package of ground R&S units as required.

(f) (U) Receive a CI element in GS.

(g) (U) Conduct preplanned and ad hoc visual aerial reconnaissance.

(h) (U) Provide remote receive station team to MEF CE.

(i) (U) Provide remote receive station team to 1st MARDIV.

(j) (U) Provide remote receive station team to 2d MARDIV.

(k) (U) Provide remote receive station team to 3d MARDIV.

(l) (U) Provide remote receive station team to 4th MARDIV.

CLASSIFICATION

CLASSIFICATION

(m) (U) Provide two-man UAV liaison teams to MEF SARC.

(n) (U) Conduct UAV displacement operations with minimal reduction of battlespace surveillance.

(o) (U) Receive ground sensor platoon liaison team to support airborne sensor implant planning.

(p) (U) Conduct airborne sensor implant when directed.

(3) (U) FSSG (-)(Reinforced)

(a) (U) Provide intelligence reporting of any enemy activity within AO to MEF G-2 operations officer.

(b) (U) Provide bridge, route, ford, and other mobility reports in accordance with reference (c) for all main/critical routes to MEF G-2 P&A cell.

(c) (U) Receive a CI element in GS.

(d) (U) Conduct ground sensor recovery operations when directed.

(4) (U) Rear Area Operations Group

(a) (U) Provide R&S reporting from adjacent headquarters/units to MEF G-2 operations officer as soon as feasible.

(b) (U) Evacuate captured personnel and materiel from the forward collection point to the central collection point by most expeditious means possible. Enforce tagging procedures in accordance with reference (b). Interrogations will only be conducted by MEF HUMINT personnel.

(c) (U) Receive a CI element in GS.

(d) (U) Conduct ground sensor recovery operations when directed.

(5) (U) Marine Engineer Group

(a) (U) Provide bridge, route, ford, and other mobility reports in accordance with reference (c) for all main/critical routes to MEF G-2 P&A cell.

(b) (U) Evacuate captured personnel and materiel from the forward collection point to the central collection point by most expeditious means possible. Enforce tagging procedures in accordance with reference (b). Interrogations will only be conducted by MEF HUMINT.

Page number

CLASSIFICATION

CLASSIFICATION

(6) (U) <u>Force Artillery Headquarters</u>

(a) (U) Provide counterfire battery radar reports to MEF SARC OIC as soon as possible.

(b) (U) Evacuate captured personnel and materiel from the forward collection point to the central collection point by most expeditious means possible. Enforce tagging procedures in accordance with reference (b). Interrogations will only be conducted by MEF HUMINT personnel.

(7) (U) <u>MEF Organic Collection Elements</u>

(a) (U) <u>Force Reconnaissance Company (-) (Reinforced)</u>

<u>1</u> (U) Implant ground sensor strings and relays as directed.

<u>2</u> (U) Provide two-man operational planning liaison team (force reconnaissance detachment) to MEF SARC.

<u>3</u> (U) Conduct simultaneous operations to support MEF Alpha and Bravo command post displacement.

<u>4</u> (U) Provide restricted fire area coordination and deconfliction of all ground R&S assets within MEF AO.

<u>5</u> (U) Provide strategic and theater ground reconnaissance planning support as required.

<u>6</u> (U) Assume operational control of selected CATF ground R&S assets postchop.

<u>7</u> (U) Engage targets of opportunity with MEF force fires authorization.

<u>8</u> (U) Provide targeting for fire support systems.

(b) (U) <u>Intelligence Battalion</u>. Provide the following R&S support:

<u>1</u> (U) <u>GSP (-) (Reinforced)</u>

<u>a</u> (U) Provide one GSP squad in DS of 1st MARDIV.

<u>b</u> (U) Provide one GSP squad in GS of 2d MARDIV.

<u>c</u> (U) Provide two-man operational planning liaison team (GSP detachment) to the MEF SARC.

<u>d</u> (U) (U) Be prepared to conduct simultaneous operations to support MEF Alpha and Bravo command post displacement.

Page number

CLASSIFICATION

CLASSIFICATION

e (U) Provide GSP liaison team to MAW for airborne sensor implant planning.

f (U) Assume operational control of selected CATF ground sensor assets postchop.

2 (U) <u>CI/HUMINT Unit</u>

a (U) Conduct CI/force protection operations in MEF AO.

b (U) Conduct HUMINT operations supporting R&S plan.

c (U) Conduct tactical interrogations to support MEF PIRs/IRs.

(c) (U) <u>Radio Battalion (-)(Reinforced)</u>

1 (U) Provide one company (1st/2d) Radio Battalion (-)(Reinforced) in DS of 1stMARDIV.

2 (U) Provide a SIGINT support platoon in GS to 2dMARDIV.

3 (U) Radio reconnaissance teams will be in DS of MEF.

4 (U) Coordinate operational planning for insertion/extraction of radio reconnaissance teams with force reconnaissance company.

5 (U) Provide two-man operational planning liaison team (radio battalion detachment) to the MEF SARC.

6 (U) Conduct simultaneous operations to support MEF Alpha and Bravo command post displacement.

7 (U) Provide electronic intelligence support for battlespace surveillance in accordance with internal SOPs.

d. (U) <u>Coordinating Instructions</u>

(1) (U) Assignment of Responsibility for Drafting of Tabs to this appendix. The MEF CM/DO will conduct a working group comprised of MSC collection requirement managers and MEF collection operation managers to discuss this appendix and to identify and assign initial responsibilities to execute this R&S plan. On completion of the working group, each command or unit responsible for the development of a supporting tab that addresses the operations management of the specific collector will draft and forward this tab to the MEF CM/DO for review and dissemination. When applicable, tabs should address the tasking, processing, exploitation, and dissemination of collected information from the collector to the MEF G-2. Command/unit responsibility for specific tabs are:

Page number

CLASSIFICATION

CLASSIFICATION

(a) (U) Tab A: SIGINT Employment Plan. MEF SIGINT officer coordinated with radio battalion.

(b) (U) Tab B: CI/HUMINT Employment Plan. MEF CI/HUMINT coordinated with intelligence battalion.

(c) (U) Tab C: Ground R&S Plan. Force Reconnaissance Company coordinated with MEF SIGINT officer.

(d) (U) Tab D: Visual Aerial Reconnaissance and Surveillance Plan. MAW.

(e) (U) Tab E: Ground Sensor Surveillance Plan. Intelligence battalion.

(f) (U) Tab F: UAV Employment Plan. MAW.

(2) (U) PIRs

(a) (U) Determine if the 7th Division will attack the MEF flank from H-Hour to H+24.

(b) (U) Determine if the 1st Armored Brigade will displace to counter amphibious landing from H-Hour To H+36.

(c) (U) Determine if the 1st Provincial Guard Corps will defend in the vicinity of Badguyburg in regiment or larger strength from H+36 To H+96.

(d) (U) As soon as practical, MSCs will identify PIRs and submit requests for collection support in accordance with this appendix.

(3) (U) IRs

(a) (U) Determine the movement of major Orange Force's units in MEF's area of responsibility.

(b) (U) Location of Orange Force's long-range artillery that can range MEF forces.

(c) (U) Projected weather conditions.

(d) (U) Any other changes to the assessed enemy COAs.

(4) (U) NAIs. (Read across Number/Location/Description/Activity)

(a) (U) 1/Grid location/southwest movement from Nashville by 1st Armored Brigade.

Page number

CLASSIFICATION

CLASSIFICATION

(b) (U) 2/Grid location/road junction Route 20/movement west of 1st Armored Brigade.

(c) (U) 3/Grid location/road junction I-95 and north/south Country Road/ movement west of 7th Division.

(d) (U) 4/Grid location/road/movement south of 1st Armored Brigade.

(e) (U) 5/Grid Location/Intersection Route 1 and Bangor Road/enemy movement southwest or southeast from Badguyburg.

(f) (U) 6/Grid location/Intersection Route 1 and Highway 101/east movement of 1st Provincial Guard Corps.

(g) (U) 7/Grid location /road junction Route 66 and unidentified road/southeast movement of 1st Provincial Guard Corps.

(5) (U) MEF CM/DO will coordinate and deconflict with higher headquarters MEF NAIs that correspond to or have been identified as a combatant commander's NAI. The MEF CM/DO will also coordinate and deconflict MEF NAIs.

(6) (U) MEF subordinate commands will prepare organic R&S plans to satisfy organic PIRs/IRs. MEF MSCs will submit organic R&S plans to the MEF CM/DO as directed.

4. (U) Logistics

5. (U) Command And Communications

   a. (U) Command

      (1) (U) Command Relationships

        (a) (U) J-2 has staff responsibility for employment of theater and national intelligence collection assets.

        (b) (U) MEF G-2 CM/DO is responsible for coordinating the employment of MEF organic R&S assets and requesting R&S support through appropriate channels to cover gaps in organic collection capability to support combatant commander and MEF PIRs.

        (c) (U) The MEF SARC is responsible for:

          1 (U) Initial planning and coordination for the operational employment of MEF organic collection assets to support this operations plan.

Page number

CLASSIFICATION

CLASSIFICATION

<u>2</u> (U) Monitoring and reporting the status and location of MEF organic collection assets

<u>3</u> (U) Collecting and reporting combat intelligence/information to the MEF P&A cell.

(d) (U) The MEF SARC OIC will assist the MEF CM/DO in developing, publishing, and revising this appendix as required.

b. (U) <u>Communications</u>. MSC R&S assets will establish communications connectivity between tasked organic units and the MEF SARC via G-2 unclassified or secret networks.

c. (U) <u>Reporting</u>. Timely reporting from organic collection operation centers via established communications paths and procedures will support reactive targeting opportunities and analysis of perishable tactical information.

d. (U) <u>Requesting Procedures</u>. Requests for intelligence support beyond the capabilities of MSCs will be submitted as a production requirement/collection requirement via the chain of command to MEF using the procedures outlined in reference (b).

APPENDIX D
SAMPLE COLLECTION STATUS UPDATE PARAGRAPH FORMAT

<u>Collection Status Update Paragraph</u>. A collection status update paragraph may be included as part of a unit's daily intelligence summary (INTSUM) in order to notify higher, adjacent, and critically, lower units of the MAGTF's current ICRs and planned collection operations over some specified future period. As a snapshot of the near term requirements, it can be used to review active and cancelled requirements and update a unit's collection priorities and collection plan daily. Using the basic format, units can tailor the INTSUM to fit the situation. With new automated information systems, INTSUMs are increasingly produced in graphic form and posted on networks for wide dissemination, with links to detailed supporting intelligence products, reports, and databases. An example of a written collection status update paragraph follows:

COLLECTION STATUS UPDATE

A. DURING THE PERIOD 040800T TO 050759T MAR 2004, THE MEF COLLECTION PRIORITIES ARE AS FOLLOWS:

PRIORITY	PIR/IR NO.	ITEM
1	1	SIGINT SUPPORT TEAM (SST) A TO EXECUTE MISSION BRAVO VIC NAI 003.
2	1	AVIATION SST UNIT TO EXECUTE MISSION CHARLIE VIC NAI 003.
3	1	AERIAL RECON MISSIONS TO PROVIDE COVERAGE OF I MEF AO ACCORDING TO AERIAL SURV PLAN (TRACKS NASHVILLE AND DAYTONA) IN MOBILITY CORRIDOR CHARLIE.
4	2	SST TEAM C TO EXECUTE MISSION ECHO VIC NAI 005.

B. CANCELLED REQUIREMENTS. THE FOLLOWING PRIORITY INTELLIGENCE REQUIREMENTS HAVE BEEN SATISFIED OR CANCELLED.

PIR NO.	DESCRIPTION
5	IMAGERY AND TEXT STUDIES OF POINT OF ENTRY VIC PORT HIDALGO. SPECIAL ATTENTION TO COASTAL LANDING BEACHES AND HELICOPTER LANDING ZONES.

C. PLANNED INTELLIGENCE COLLECTION MISSIONS. THE FOLLOWING MEF INTELLIGENCE COLLECTION MISSIONS ARE PLANNED FOR EXECUTION DURING THE PERIOD 050800T TO 060759T MAR 2004.

PRIORITY	PIR/IR NO.	ITEM
1	2	EA-6B/PROWLER UNIT A TO COLLECT IAW TASKING PER AIR TASKING ORDER.
2	3	HELO INSERTION OF GROUND RECON TEAM 111 INTO RESTRICTED AREA OF OPERATIONS 111 VIC NAI 006.
3	3	3RD GSP TO CONDUCT SENSOR EMPLACEMENT OPERATIONS IN MOBILITY CORRIDOR MESA.

APPENDIX E
SAMPLE COLLECTION EMPHASIS MESSAGE

FM CG I MEF//G2//CMDO//

TO CG FIRST MARDIV//G2/CM//

CG FIRST FSSG//G2/CM//

CG THIRD MAW//G2/CM//

INFO CG II MEF//G2/CM//

CG III MEF//G2/CM

CJTF BLUE

UNCLAS N03800//

EXERCISE EXERCISE EXERCISE

MSGID/CEM/I MEF G2/001//

SUBJ/COLLECTION EMPHASIS MESSAGE//

REF/A/DOC/I MEF EXERCISE OPORD 04

REF/B/MAP/NIMA/-//

NARR/REF A IS I MEF OPORD FOR EXERCISE 04. APP 1, ANNEX B, CONTAINS MEF PIRS FOR EXERCISE. REF B ARE MAPS FOR EXERCISE AREAS; SERIES, SHEETS, EDITION AND SCALE//

POC/BOSS, I.M./MAJ/USMC/CMDO/DSN 492-0283//

RMKS/1. (U) AS DISSEMINATED IN REF A, THE FOLLOWING PIRS ARE THE FOCUS OF I MEF G2 INTELLIGENCE COLLECTION STRATEGY DURING PHASE ONE OF THE EXERCISE. REQUEST WIDEST DISSEMINATION OF THESE PIRS TO ALL SUBORDINATE UNITS.

2. (U) PIR 1. WILL 3D ARMOR DIV CROSS LINE OF DEPARTURE PRIOR TO I MEF AMPHIB ASSLT ON D PLUS FOUR.

A. SIGINT. REPORT INCREASE IN ENEMY COMMS BTWN 3D ARMOR DIV UNITS. SPECIFIC ATTN TO COMMS BTWN HQ, 3D ARMOR DIV AND HQ, 4TH CORPS. PROVIDE INDICATIONS AND WARNING OF ENEMY APPROACH VIC NAIS 001, 002.

B. IMINT. PROVIDE COVERAGE OF I MEF AO ACCORDING TO PRIORITIZED IMAGERY TARGET LIST.

C. GROUND RECON. REPORT ENEMY ACTIVITY IN VIC NAIS 001, 002. REPORT LOCATION, NUMBER, HEADING AND SPEED OF VEHICLES.

D. AERIAL RECON. PROVIDE COVERAGE OF I MEF AO ACCORDING TO AERIAL SURV PLAN (TRACKS NASHVILLE AND LINCOLN) IN MOBILITY CORRIDORS LAVA AND DELTA. REPORT LOCATION, NUMBER, HEADING, AND SPEED OF VEHICLES.

E. HUMINT. REPORT INDICATIONS OF 3D ARMOR DIV PLANS TO DEPLOY.

F. CI. REPORT INDICATIONS OF ENEMY ACTIVITY IN I MEF AO. SPECIFIC ATTN TO BEACH SUPPORT AREA (NAI 004).

G. MASINT. CONDUCT SENSOR MONITORING AND REPORTING TO PROVIDE I&W OF ENEMY ACTIVITY IN MOBILITY CORRIDORS LAVA AND DELTA. REPORT ENEMY ACTIVITY. DETERMINE NUMBER, TYPE, HEADING, AND SPEED OF VEHICLES.

3. (U) PIR 2. WILL 4TH CORPS RESERVE DEPLOY TO ASSEMBLY AREA (AA) MULE PRIOR TO D PLUS FOUR.

A. SIGINT. REPORT INCREASE IN ENEMY COMMS BY AND BTWN 11 MECH INF BDE. SPECIFIC ATTN TO COMMS BTWN HQ, 11 MECH INF BDE AND HQ, 4TH CORPS. PROVIDE I&W OF ENEMY APPROACH VIC NAIS 006, 007.

B. IMINT. PROVIDE COVERAGE OF I MEF AO ACCORDING TO PRIORITIZED IMAGERY LIST.

C. GROUND RECON. REPORT ENEMY ACTIVITY IN VIC NAIS 006, 007. REPORT LOCATION, NUMBER, HEADING, AND SPEED OF VEHICLES.

D. AERIAL RECON. PROVIDE COVERAGE OF I MEF AO ACCORDING TO AERIAL SURV PLAN (TRACKS KNOXVILLE AND OMAHA) IN MOBILITY CORRIDOR MAIN. REPORT LOCATION, NUMBER, HEADING, AND SPEED OF VEHICLES.

E. HUMINT. REPORT INDICATIONS OF 11TH MECH INF BDE PLANS TO DEPLOY TO AA MULE.

F. CI.

G. MASINT. CONDUCT SENSOR MONITORING AND REPORTING TO PROVIDE I&W OF ENEMY ACTIVITY IN MOBILITY CORRIDOR MAIN. REPORT ENEMY ACTIVITY. DETERMINE NUMBER, TYPE, HEADING, AND SPEED OF VEHICLES.

4. (U) PIR 3. WILL 4TH CORPS EMPLOY NUCLEAR, BIOLOGICAL OR CHEMICAL (NBC) WEAPONS IN THE VICINITY OF THE LANDING BEACHES DURING I MEF AMPHIB ASSLT.

A. SIGINT. REPORT INDICATIONS OF ENEMY USE OR EMPLOYMENT OF NBC WEAPONS. SPECIFIC ATTN TO HQ, 4TH CORPS COMMS. PROVIDE I&W OF NBC EMPLOYMENT VIC NAI 004.

B. IMINT.

C. GROUND RECON. REPORT INDICATIONS THAT ENEMY IS PREPARING TO EMPLOY NBC WEAPONS WITHIN MEF AO. SPECIFIC ATTN TO ENEMY GROUND FORCE UNITS ISSUING NBC PROTECTIVE GEAR.

D. AERIAL RECON.

E. HUMINT. REPORT INDICATIONS THAT ENEMY IS PREPARING TO EMPLOY NBC WEAPONS WITHIN MEF AO. SPECIFIC ATTN TO CIVIL MEASURES OR PREPARATIONS FOR NBC EMPLOYMENT.

F. CI. REPORT INDICATIONS THAT ENEMY IS PREPARING TO EMPLOY NBC WEAPONS WITHIN MEF AO. SPECIFIC ATTN TO CIVIL MEASURES OR PREPARATIONS FOR NBC EMPLOYMENT.

G. MASINT.

5. (U) PLANNED INTELLIGENCE COLLECTION MISSIONS FOR THE PERIOD 040800T TO 060759T MAR 04 ARE AS FOLLOWS (REFERENCE MEF COLLECTION PLAN ON THE MEF S-TDN WEB SITE.)

A. SIGINT. SST TEAM A TO EXECUTE MISSION BRAVO VIC NAI 003. AVIATION SST UNIT C TO EXECUTE MISSION CHARLIE VIC NAI 003.

EA-6B/PROWLER UNIT A TO COLLECT AGAINST PIR #2 (TASKING PER ITO/ATO).

B. IMINT.

C. GROUND RECON. HELO INSERTION OF TEAM 111 INTO RAO 111 VIC NAI 006.

D. AERIAL RECON. PROVIDE COVERAGE OF I MEF AO ACCORDING TO AERIAL SURV PLAN (TRACKS NASHVILLE AND DAYTONA) IN MOBILITY CORRIDOR CHARLIE.

E. HUMINT.

F. CI.

G. MASINT. 3D GSP TO CONDUCT SENSOR EMPLACEMENT OPERATIONS INMOBILITY CORRIDOR MESA.

6. (U) UPDATES TO THE COLLECTION STRATEGY WILL BE DISSEMINATED IN COLLECTION STATUS UPDATE PARAGRAPH OF MEF INTSUMS, ON-LINE VIA MEF GRAPHICAL COLLECTION PLAN ON THE MEF S-TDN WEB SITE, AND IN FUTURE COLLECTION EMPHASIS MESSAGES.

BT

#0001

NNNN

APPENDIX F
GLOSSARY

SECTION I
ACRONYMS AND ABBREVIATIONS

AO . . . . area of operations
ATARS . . . . advanced tactical airborne
reconnaissance system

BDA . . . . battle damage assessment

C2 . . . . command and control
CATF . . . . . . commander, amphibious task force
CE . . . . command element
CI . . . . counterintelligence
CIS . . . communications and information systems
CLF . . . . commander, landing force
CM/DO . . . . collection management/
dissemination officer
COA . . . . course of action
COM . . . . .collection operations management
COMINT . . . . communications intelligence
COP . . . . common operational picture
CRM . . . . . collection requirements management
CTP . . . . common tactical picture

DIAM . . . . Defense Intelligence Agency Manual
DODIPP . . . Department of Defense Intelligence
Production Program
DS . . . . direct support

ELINT . . . . electronic intelligence
EW .electronic warfare

FRAGO . . . . .fragmentary order
FSSG . . . . force service support group

G-2 . . . . intelligence staff officer
(brigade or higher)
G-3 . . . . operations staff officer
G-5 . . . . plans staff officer
GIRH . . . . generic intelligence
requirements handbook

GS . . . . general support
GSP . . . . ground sensor platoon

HET . . . . .HUMINT exploitation team
HUMINT . . . . human intelligence

ICR . . . . intelligence collection requirement
IDR . . . . . intelligence dissemination requirement
IMINT . . . . .imagery intelligence
INTSUM . . . . intelligence summary
IOC . . . . .intelligence operations center
IPB . . .intelligence preparation of the battlespace
IPR . . . . . . intelligence production requirement
IR . . . . .intelligence requirement
ISC . . . . intelligence support coordinator

J-2 . . . . intelligence directorate of a joint staff
JP . . . . .joint publication
JSTARS . . . . joint surveillance target
attack radar system
JTF . . . . joint task force

LOC . . . . line of communications
LTIOV . . . . . . latest time intelligence is of value

MAGTF . . . . Marine air-ground task force
MARDIV . . . . Marine division
MASINT . . . . measurement and signature
intelligence
MAW . . . . .Marine aircraft wing
MCDP . . . . . . Marine Corps doctrinal publication
MCIA . . . . . . Marine Corps Intelligence Activity
MCRP . . . . . .Marine Corps reference publication
MCWP . . .Marine Corps warfighting publication
MEF . . . . Marine expeditionary force
mm . . . . .millimeter
MSC . . . . major subordinate command

NAI . . . . named area of interest

OIC . . . . officer in charge
OPLAN . . . . .operation plan
OPORD . . . . operation order
OSINT . . . . open-source intelligence

P&A . . . . production and analysis
PIR . . . . priority intelligence requirement
PR . . . . production request

R&S . . . . reconnaissance and surveillance
RadBn . . . . radio battalion
RECON . . . . reconnaissance
RFI . . . . .request for intelligence

S-2 . . . . intelligence staff officer
(battalion or regiment)
S-3 . . . . plans staff officer
(battalion or regiment)
SARC . . . . . surveillance and reconnaissance cell

SIGINT . . . . .signals intelligence
SII . . . . statement of intelligence interest
SIR . . . . .specific information requirement
SOP . . . . .standing operating procedure
SOR . . . . .specific order or request
SST . . . . .SIGINT support team
SSU . . . . SIGINT support unit

TTP . . . . tactics, techniques, and procedures

UAV . . . . .unmanned aerial vehicle

VIC . . . . vicinity
VMAQ . . . . .Marine tactical electronic
warfare squadron
VMU . . . . .Marine unmanned aerial
vehicle squadron
VO . . . . validation officer

SECTION II
DEFINITIONS

area of operations—An operational area defined by the joint force commander for land and naval forces. Areas of operation do not typically encompass the entire operational area of the joint force commander, but should be large enough for component commanders to accomplish their missions and protect their forces. Also called **AO**. (JP 1-02)

battle damage assessment—The timely and accurate estimate of damage resulting from the application of military force, either lethal or non-lethal, against a predetermined objective. Battle damage assessment can be applied to the employment of all types of weapon systems (air, ground, naval, and special forces weapon systems) throughout the range of military operations. Battle damage assessment is primarily an intelligence responsibility with required inputs and coordination from the operators. Battle damage assessment is composed of physical damage assessment, functional damage assessment, and target system assessment. (JP 1-

02) In Marine Corps usage, the timely and accurate estimate of the damage resulting from the application of military force. BDA estimates physical damage to a particular target, functional damage to that target, and the capability of the entire target system to continue its operations. Also called **BDA**. (MCRP 5-12C)

collection—Acquisition of information and the provision of this information to processing (JP 1-02) In Marine Corps usage, the gathering of intelligence data and information to satisfy the identified requirements. (MCRP 5-12C)

collection management—In intelligence usage, the process of converting intelligence requirements into collection requirements, establishing priorities, tasking or coordinating with appropriate collection sources or agencies, monitoring results and retasking, as required. (JP 1-02)

collection operations management—The authoritative direction, scheduling, and control of specific collection operations and associated processing, exploitation, and reporting resources. Also called **COM**. (JP 1-02)

collection plan—A plan for collecting information from all available sources to meet intelligence requirements and for transforming those requirements into orders and requests to appropriate agencies. (JP 1-02)

collection requirement—An established intelligence need considered in the allocation of intelligence resources to fulfill the priority intelligence requirements and other intelligence needs of a commander. (This definition modifies the JP 1-02 entry and will be included in the next edition of MCRP 5-12C.)

collection requirements management—The authoritative development and control of collection, processing, exploitation, and/or reporting requirements that normally result in either direct tasking of assets over which the collection manager has authority, or the generation of tasking requests to collection management authorities at a higher, lower, or lateral echelon to accomplish the collection mission. Also called **CRM**. (JP 1-02)

combatant command—A unified or specified command with a broad continuing mission under a single commander established and so designated by the President, through the Secretary of Defense and with the advice and assistance of the Chairman of the Joint Chiefs of Staff. Combatant commands typically have geographic or functional responsibilities. (JP 1-02)

command and control—The exercise of authority and direction by a properly designated commander over assigned and attached forces in the accomplishment of the mission. Command and control functions are performed through an arrangement of personnel, equipment, communications, facilities, and procedures employed by a commander in planning, directing, coordinating, and controlling forces and operations in the accomplishment of the mission. (JP 1-02) Also in Marine Corps usage, the means by which a commander recognizes what needs to be done and sees to it that appropriate actions are taken. Also called **C2**. (MCRP 5-12C)

command element—The core element of a Marine air-ground task force (MAGTF) that is the headquarters. The command element (CE) is composed of the commander, general or executive and special staff sections, headquarters section, and requisite communications support, intelligence and reconnaissance forces, necessary to accomplish the MAGTF's mission. The CE provides command and control, intelligence, and other support essential for effective planning and execution of operations by the other elements of the MAGTF. The CE varies in size and composition and may contain other Service or foreign military forces assigned or attached to the MAGTF. Also called **CE**. (This definition modifies the JP 1-02 entry and will be included in the next edition of MCRP 5-12C.)

counterintelligence—1. Information gathered and activities conducted to protect against espionage, other intelligence activities, sabotage, or assassinations conducted by or on behalf of foreign governments or elements thereof, foreign organizations, or foreign persons, or international terrorist activities. (JP 1-02) 2. Within the Marine Corps, counterintelligence constitutes active and passive measures intended to deny a threat force valuable information about the friendly situation, to detect and neutralize hostile intelligence collection, and to deceive the enemy as to friendly capabilities and intentions. Also called **CI**. (MCRP 5-12C)

dissemination—Conveyance of intelligence to users in a suitable form. (JP 1-02)

dissemination management—Involves establishing dissemination priorities, selection of dissemination means, and monitoring the flow of intelligence throughout the command. The objective of dissemination management is to deliver the required intelligence to the appropriate user in proper form at the right time while ensuring that individual consumers and the dissemination system are not overloaded attempting to move unneeded or irrelevant information. Dissemination management also provides for use of security controls which do not impede the timely delivery or subsequent use of intelligence while protecting intelligence sources and methods. (MCRP 5-12C)

force protection—Actions taken to prevent or mitigate hostile actions against Department of Defense personnel (to include family members), resources, facilities, and critical information. These actions conserve the force's fighting potential so it can be applied at the decisive time and place and incorporate the coordinated and synchronized offensive and defensive measures to enable the effective employment of the joint force while degrading opportunities for the enemy. Force protection does not include actions to defeat the enemy or protect against accidents, weather, or disease. (JP 1-02)

geographic intelligence—The process of collecting, organizing, analyzing, synthesizing, disseminating, and using all-source geospatial and other intelligence information with regard to the military aspects of the terrain in support of MAGTF operations. (MCWP 2-12.1)

human intelligence—A category of intelligence derived from information collected and provided by human sources. (JP1-02) In Marine Corps usage, human intelligence operations cover a wide range of activities encompassing reconnaissance patrols, aircrew reports and debriefs, debriefing of refugees, interrogations of prisoners of war, and the conduct of counterintelligence force protection source operations. Also called **HUMINT.** (MCRP 5-12C)

imagery intelligence—Intelligence derived from the exploitation of collection by visual photography, infrared sensors, lasers, electro-optics, and radar sensors such as synthetic aperture radar wherein images of objects are reproduced optically or electronically on film, electronic display devices, or other media. Also called **IMINT**. (JP 1-02)

indications and warning—Those intelligence activities intended to detect and report time-sensitive intelligence information on foreign developments that could involve a threat to the United States or allied and/or coalition military, political, or economic interests or to US citizens abroad. It includes forewarning of enemy actions or intentions; the imminence of hostilities; insurgency; nuclear or non-nuclear attack on the United States, its overseas forces, or allied and/or coalition nations; hostile reactions to US reconnaissance activities; terrorists' attacks; and other similar events. Also called **I&W**. (JP 1-02)

indications (intelligence)—Information in various degrees of evaluation, all of which bear on the intention of a potential enemy to adopt or reject a course of action. (JP 1-02)

indicator—In intelligence usage, an item of information which reflects the intention or capability of a potential enemy to adopt or reject a course of action. (JP 1-02)

intelligence—1. The product resulting from the collection, processing, integration, analysis, evaluation, and interpretation of available information concerning foreign countries or areas. 2. Information and knowledge about an adversary obtained through observation, investigation, analysis, or understanding. (JP 1-02) Also in Marine Corps usage, intelligence is knowledge about the enemy or the surrounding environment needed to support decisionmaking. This knowledge is the result of the collection, processing, exploitation, evaluation, integration, analysis, and interpretation of available information about the battlespace and threat. (MCRP 5-12C)

intelligence cycle—A six-step process by which information is converted into intelligence and made available to users. The six steps are planning and direction, collection, processing and exploitation, production, dissemination, and utilization. (MCWP 2-1) (This definition modifies the JP 1-02 entry and will be included in the next edition of MCRP 5-12C.)

intelligence preparation of the battlespace—An analytical methodology employed to reduce uncertainties concerning the enemy, environment, and terrain for all types of operations. Intelligence preparation of the battlespace builds an extensive database for each potential area in which a unit may be required to operate. The database is then analyzed in detail to determine the impact of the enemy, environment, and terrain on operations and presents it in graphic form. Intelligence preparation of the battlespace is a continuing process. (JP 1-02) In Marine Corps usage, the systematic, continuous process of analyzing the threat and environment in a specific geographic area. Also called **IPB**. (MCRP 5-12C)

intelligence report—A specific report of information, usually on a single item, made at any level of command in tactical operations and disseminated as rapidly as possible in keeping with the timeliness of the information. Also called **INTREP**. (JP 1-02)

intelligence requirement—1. Any subject, general or specific, upon which there is a need for the collection of information, or the production of intelligence. 2. A requirement for intelligence to fill a gap in the command's knowledge or understanding of the battlespace or threat forces. (JP 1-02) In Marine Corps usage, questions about the enemy and the environment, the answers to which a commander requires to make sound decisions. Also called **IR**. (MCRP 5-12C)

joint intelligence center—The intelligence center of the combatant command headquarters. The joint intelligence center is responsible for providing and producing the intelligence required to support the combatant commander and staff, components, subordinate joint forces and elements, and the national intelligence community. Also called **JIC**. (JP 1-02)

Marine air-ground task force—The Marine Corps principal organization for all missions across the range of military operations, composed of forces task-organized under a single commander capable of responding rapidly to a contingency anywhere in the world. The types of forces in the Marine air-ground task force (MAGTF) are functionally grouped into four core elements: a command element, an aviation combat element, a ground combat element, and a combat service support element. The four core elements are categories of forces, not formal commands. The basic structure of the MAGTF never varies, though the number, size, and type of Marine Corps units comprising each of its four elements will always be mission dependent. The flexibility of the organizational structure allows for one or more subordinate MAGTFs, other Service, and/or foreign military forces to be assigned or attached. Also called **MAGTF**. (This definition modifies the JP 1-02 entry and will be included in the next edition of MCRP 5-12C.)

Marine expeditionary force—The largest Marine air-ground task force (MAGTF) and the Marine Corps principal warfighting organization, particularly for larger crises or contingencies. It is task-organized around a permanent command element and normally contains one or more Marine divisions, Marine aircraft wings, and Marine force service support groups. The Marine expeditionary force is capable of missions across the range of military operations, including amphibious assault and sustained operations ashore in any environment. It can operate from a sea base, a land base, or both. It may also contain other Service or foreign military forces assigned or attached. Also called **MEF**. (This definition modifies the JP 1-02 entry and will be included in the next edition of MCRP 5-12C.)

measurement and signature intelligence—Scientific and technical intelligence obtained by quantitative and qualitative analysis of data (metric, angle, spatial, wavelength, time dependence, modulation, plasma, and hydromagnetic) derived from specific technical sensors for the purpose of identifying any distinctive features associated with the target, source emitter, or sender measurement of the same. The detected feature may be either reflected or emitted. Also called **MASINT**. (JP 1-02)

priority intelligence requirements—Those intelligence requirements for which a commander has an anticipated and stated priority in the task of planning and decisionmaking. (JP 1-02) In Marine Corps usage, an intelligence requirement associated with a decision that will critically affect the overall success of the command's mission. Also called **PIRs**. (MCRP 5-12C)

signals intelligence—1. A category of intelligence comprising either individually or in combination all communications intelligence, electronic intelligence, and foreign instrumentation signals intelligence, however transmitted. 2. Intelligence derived from communications, electronic, and foreign instrumentation signals. Also called **SIGINT**. (JP 1-02)

split base—Two or more portions of the same force conducting or supporting operations from separate physical locations. (MCRP 5-12C)

surveillance and reconnaissance cell—Primary element responsible for the supervision of MAGTF intelligence collection operations. Directs, coordinates, and monitors intelligence collection operations conducted by organic, attached, and direct support collection assets. Also called **SARC**. (Change approved for inclusion in the next version of MCRP 5-12C.)

validation—A process normally associated with the collection of intelligence that provides official status to an identified requirement and confirms that the requirement is appropriate for a given collector and has not been previously satisfied. (JP 1-02 part 1)

APPENDIX G
REFERENCES

Department of Defense Publications

Defense Intelligence Management Document 0000-151C-95, *Department of Defense Intelligence Production Program (DODIPP): Production Procedures (U)*

Defense Intelligence Agency Manual 57-05, *DOD Exploitation of Multi-Sensor Imagery*

Joint Publications (JPs)

1-02	Department of Defense Dictionary of Military and Associated Terms
2-0	Doctrine for Intelligence Support to Joint Operations
2-01	Joint Intelligence Support to Military Operations

Marine Corps Doctrinal Publications (MCDPs)

2	Intelligence
5	Planning

Marine Corps Warfighting Publications (MCWPs)

2-1	Intelligence Operations
2-12	MAGTF Intelligence Production and Analysis
2-14	Counterintelligence
2-15.1	Remote Sensor Operations
2-15.2	Signals Intelligence
2-15.4	Imagery Intelligence
3-26	Air Reconnaissance
3-40.1	Marine Air-Ground Task Force Command and Control
3-40.5	Electronic Warfare
3-42.1	Unmanned Aerial Vehicle Operations
5-1	Marine Corps Planning Process

Marine Corps Reference Publications (MCRPs)

2-12A   Intelligence Preparation of the Battlefield
2-15.3B   Reconnaissance Reports Guide
5-12C   Marine Corps Supplement to the DOD Dictionary of Military and Associated Terms

Marine Corps Intelligence Activity (MCIA) Publication

1540-002-95   Generic Intelligence Requirements Handbook (GIRH)

Army Field Manual (FM)

34-2   Collection Management and Synchronization Planning